GW00374253

John's Gospel
a bite-sized chunk of the **Bible.**
New International Version

Hodder & Stoughton

LONDON SYDNEY AUCKLAND

Designed and illustrated by Well Outpoured Design, Dorchester, Dorset.
Printed and bound in Great Britain by Ebenezer Baylis, Worcester for Hodder and Stoughton Ltd, a member of the Hodder Headline Group, 338 Euston Road, London NW1 3BH

what can we say but...

thanks to

and in order of appearance

God the Father
God the Son
God the Holy Spirit

Peter Duke - Bible Society
Elaine Williams - Crusaders
Liz Biddulph, David Westlake - Soul Survivor
Roy Crown - B.Y.F.C.
Peter Ward - Oxford Youth Works
Tim Carr - Bible Society
Emma Sealey, James Catford, Charles Nettleton,
    Tim Moyler - Hodder & Stoughton Ltd
Craig Borlase - Soul Survivor
Directors of W J White and Sons Ltd
New Covenant Church, Weymouth
John & Maureen Darmanin
Dave and Sally Scragg
Christine Dyer - Derby Youth Officer
Karina Green - Diocesan Youth Officer
Peter Ball - National Youth Officer
J. John, Martyn Day - Philo Trust
Mike and Ruth Robbins
Tim Dawkins - TD Photography
Mike Pilavachi - Soul Survivor
Martin Selman - Spurgeon's College
The crew - Chris & Ruth, Kay, Jan, Caroline,
Clive, Steve & Janine, Hazel, Chrissy, Theresa,
Dotty, Naomi, David & Joy, Winnie.

Proverbs 31:10

Anna
with Joshua & Emily

Wendy

You by your love
released us to do all
that was required.
xx

Well Outpoured Design:
Andrew Darmanin and Paul White.

Andrew is a graphic designer who's also pretty much involved with youth work and church stuff generally. Paul is a pastor and a fine artist. We work together to get people in touch with Jesus in whatever way we can.

Contents...

How to use this book

Well, we hope you'll read it!! - make us feel wanted!
If you do read it, it will be like a key to unlock the
rest of the Bible.

The Bible text used is the 100% fruity **New
International Version**, which a whole bunch of
wonderful scholars and proffs put together in 1979
after 11+ years of solid work!

"a sample page to highlight the many helpful features you will find in "read this"

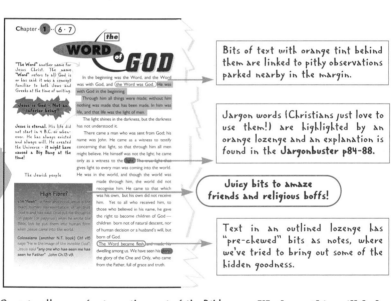

Bits of text with orange tint behind them are linked to pithy observations parked nearby in the margin.

Jargon words (Christians just love to use them!) are highlighted by an orange lozenge and an explanation is found in the **Jargonbuster p84-88**.

Juicy bits to amaze friends and religious boffs!

Text in an outlined lozenge has "pre-chewed" bits as notes, where we've tried to bring out some of the hidden goodness.

Occasionally we refer to another part of the Bible eg,

1 Corinthians Ch 13 v6

| Book number
| | Book name
| | | Chapter 13
| | | | Verse 6

**We hope this will help
you get interested in
the whole Bible.**

Also
O.T. - Old Testament
N.T. - New Testament

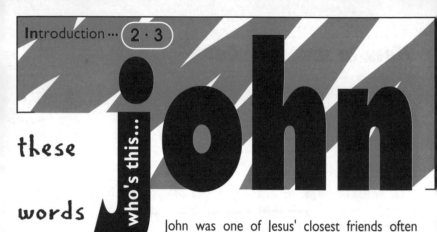

who's this...

john

these

words

are

written

that you

may

believe

John was one of Jesus' closest friends often called "the disciple whom Jesus loved". John and his brother James were fishermen, sharing the business with their father Zebedee, (real name!!). They suddenly packed in fishing one day when Jesus walked by and asked them to follow him. He called them the "**sons of thunder**," maybe they were just "**happening**" people! Jesus and his team enjoyed some fun together, they were nothing like as boring as stained glass windows have left us believing!

Apart from Judas, who had a nasty run-in with a piece of rope (Matthew Ch 27 v5), John was the only one of the apostles who was not martyred. He was exiled as an old man however and sent to the island of Patmos because of his faith. While living on this remote island, away from it all, he saw an amazing vision of Jesus

that Jesus is the Christ

he's my mate...

which he wrote down and which has become known as **"The Book of Revelation"**. The last book in the Bible

Why did he write this book?

John was so close to Jesus that he captures details not brought out in the other three Gospels, Matthew, Mark and Luke. He gives us his own special reason for writing the book:

Chapter 20 verses 30, 31.

"Jesus did many other miraculous signs in the presence of his disciples, which are not recorded in this book. But these are written that you may believe that Jesus is the Christ, the Son of God, and that by believing you may have life in his name."

John wrote his book to spell out that Jesus is not only an outstanding man, not only sent from God, but God himself.

A major theme of John's Gospel is **life: Ch 10 v10...** "I have come that they may have life, and have it to the full". Look out for the "pointy-finger" icon, pointing to life.

patmos
famous for Revelation

state of the play

Jesus was born a Jew. His country was under Roman occupation at the time, which had advantages and disadvantages. The good bit was that the roads were pretty hot - communication was exploding worldwide. The downer was that you had to pay loads of tax to Caesar.

The Jews had been longing for the "Messiah" for ages. They thought he would get them out from under the jack-boot of the Romans, but God had another plan. Enter Jesus…

jesus' boyhood

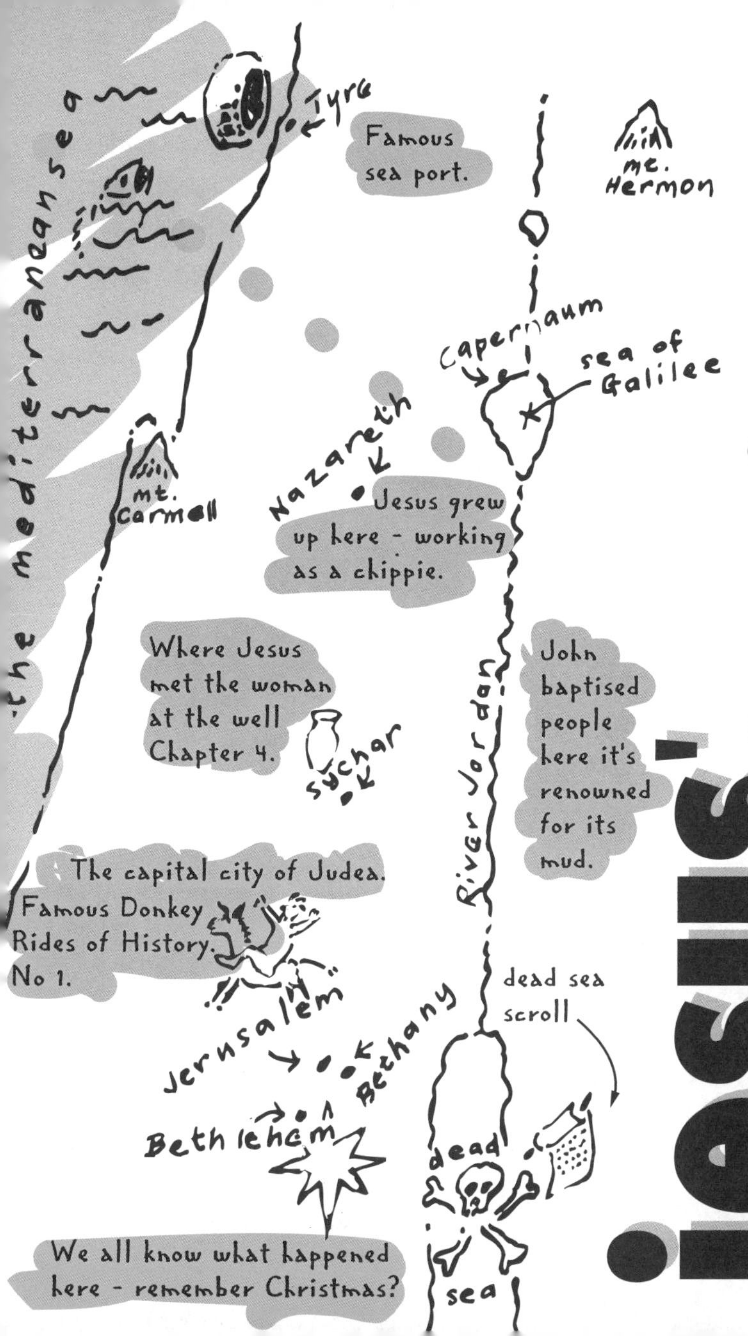

the WORD of GOD

chapter 1

"The Word" another name for Jesus Christ. The name **"Word"** refers to all God is or has said: it was a concept familiar to both Jews and Greeks at the time of writing.

Jesus is God - Not an inferior being!!

Jesus is eternal. His life did not start in 4 B.C. or whenever. He has always existed and always will. He created the Universe - it might have caused a Big Bang at the time!

The Jewish people

High Fibre?

v14 "flesh" - ie flesh and blood. Jesus is the exact human representation of all that God is and has said. God put his thoughts on paper (or papyrus) when he inspired the writers of the Bible, but he put them into human form when Jesus came into the world.

Colossians (another N.T. book) Ch 1 v15 tells us "He is the image of the invisible God"; Jesus said **"any one who has seen me has seen the Father"** John Ch 14 v9.

In the beginning was the Word, and the Word was with God, and the Word was God. [2] He was with God in the beginning.

[3] Through him all things were made; without him nothing was made that has been made. [4] In him was life, and that life was the light of men. [5] The light shines in the darkness, but the darkness has not understood it.

[6] There came a man who was sent from God; his name was John. [7] He came as a witness to testify concerning that light, so that through him all men might believe. [8] He himself was not the light; he came only as a witness to the light. [9] The true light that gives light to every man was coming into the world.

[10] He was in the world, and though the world was made through him, the world did not recognise him.

[11] He came to that which was his own, but his own did not receive him. [12] Yet to all who received him, to those who believed in his name, he gave the right to become children of God —[13] children born not of natural descent, nor of human decision or a husband's will, but born of God.

[14] The Word became flesh and made his dwelling among us. We have seen his glory, the glory of the One and Only, who came from the Father, full of grace and truth.

[15] John testifies concerning him. He cries out, saying, "This was he of whom I said, 'He who comes after me has surpassed me because he was before me.' " [16] From the fulness of his grace we have all received one blessing after another. [17] For the law was given through Moses; grace and truth came through Jesus Christ. [18] No-one has ever seen God, but God the One and Only, who is at the Father's side, has made him known.

Although John was born before Jesus (they were cousins), Jesus has always existed.

Another name for Jesus who is a "one-off"!

[19] Now this was John's testimony when the Jews of Jerusalem sent priests and Levites to ask him who he was. [20] He did not fail to confess, but confessed freely, "I am not the Christ."

[21] They asked him, "Then who are you? Are you Elijah?"

He said, "I am not."

"Are you the Prophet?"

He answered, "No."

[22] Finally they said, "Who are you? Give us an answer to take back to those who sent us. What do you say about yourself?"

[23] John replied in the words of Isaiah the prophet, "I am the voice of one calling in the desert, 'Make straight the way for the Lord.' "

[24] Now some Pharisees who had been sent [25] questioned him, "Why then do you baptise if you are not the Christ, nor Elijah, nor the Prophet?"

[26] "I baptise with water," John replied, "but among you stands one you do not know. [27] He is the one who comes after me, the thongs of whose sandals I am not worthy to untie."

[28] This all happened at Bethany on the other side of the Jordan, where John was baptising.

John did fulfil some of the prophecy regarding the return of Elijah (O.T. Book of Malachi Ch 4 v5). His role was to prepare people's hearts for Jesus.

Jesus the Lamb of God

²⁹ The next day John saw Jesus coming towards him and said, "Look, (the Lamb of God,) who takes away the sin of the world! ³⁰ This is the one I meant when I said, 'A man who comes after me has surpassed me because (he was before me.) ³¹ I myself did not know him, but the reason I came baptising with water was that he might be revealed to Israel."

³² Then John gave this testimony: "I saw the Spirit come down from heaven as a dove and remain on him. ³³ I would not have known him, except that the one who sent me to baptise with water told me, 'The man on whom you see the Spirit come down and remain is he who will baptise with the Holy Spirit.' ³⁴ I have seen and I testify that this is the Son of God."

³⁵ The next day John was there again with two of his disciples. ³⁶ When he saw Jesus passing by, he said, "Look, the Lamb of God!"

³⁷ When the two disciples heard him say this, they followed Jesus. ³⁸ Turning round, Jesus saw them following and asked, "What do you want?"

They said, "Rabbi" (which means Teacher), "where are you staying?"

³⁹"Come," he replied, "and you will see."

So they went and saw where he was staying, and spent that day with him. It was about the tenth hour.

⁴⁰Andrew, Simon Peter's brother, was one of the two who heard what John had said and who had followed Jesus. ⁴¹The first thing Andrew did was to find his brother Simon and tell him, "We have found the Messiah" (that is, the Christ). ⁴²And he brought him to Jesus.

Jesus looked at him and said, "You are Simon son

High Fibre?

v29. "The Lamb of God" - refers to the O.T. practice of sacrificing lambs etc. for sin. **Jesus came** to pay for the sin of all mankind by giving his own life as the ultimate sacrifice. **The penalty for sin is death. See Ch 3.**

Again as in v15, John spells it out about Jesus' eternal nature: his "pre-existence"

Andrew spent **one day** with Jesus and knew instantly he was the **Messiah** (JB) - the one every Israelite was waiting for!

of John. You will be called Cephas" (which, when translated, is Peter).

Simon means "Reed" - bendy, Peter means "Rock" - steady!

⁴³ The next day Jesus decided to leave for Galilee. Finding Philip, he said to him, "Follow me."

⁴⁴ Philip, like Andrew and Peter, was from the town of Bethsaida. ⁴⁵Philip found Nathanael and told him, "We have found the one (Moses) wrote about in (the Law), and about whom the prophets also wrote—Jesus of Nazareth, the son of Joseph."

⁴⁶ "Nazareth! Can anything good come from there?" Nathanael asked.

"Come and see," said Philip.

⁴⁷ When Jesus saw Nathanael approaching, he said of him, "Here is a true Israelite, in whom there is nothing false."

⁴⁸ "How do you know me?" Nathanael asked.

Jesus answered, "I saw you while you were still under the fig-tree before Philip called you."

⁴⁹Then Nathanael declared, "Rabbi, you are the Son of God; you are the King of Israel."

⁵⁰ Jesus said, "You believe because I told you I saw you under the fig-tree. You shall see greater things than that." ⁵¹ He then added, "I tell you the truth, you shall see heaven open, and the angels of God ascending and descending on the Son of Man."

"Come and see" - That's the best thing to say to other people when God has touched your life - "come see for yourself"!

v48 & 51 Jesus said "Blessed are the pure in heart, for they will see God" Matthew Ch 5 v8

John T' Bap.

Was not your average Sunday school teacher type of bloke! In fact, he looked pretty wild, wearing camel skins and eating creepy crawly locusts! Yuk!!

God often uses people or methods which offend our sense of respectability - after all, Jesus was born in a skanky old cow shed!

John was the last of the Old Testament prophets. He had the awesome job of actually saying **"this is the One"** (**"Look the Lamb of God"** - v36). He had to be 100% accurate - good job he didn't point to Judas by mistake!

Want to find out more about John the Baptist? Read Matthew Ch 3, Mark Ch 1 and Luke Ch 3.

chapter 2

Wedding *Feast.*

The Holy Spirit -ⓙⒷ is compared to wine - the disciples appeared drunk at Pentecost in the book of Acts Ch 2!

(Good Motto)

On the third day a wedding took place at Cana in Galilee. Jesus' mother was there, [2] and Jesus and his disciples had also been invited to the wedding. [3] When the wine was gone, Jesus' mother said to him, "They have no more wine."

[4] "Dear woman, why do you involve me?" Jesus replied. "My time has not yet come."

[5] His mother said to the servants, ("Do whatever he tells you.")

[6] Nearby stood six stone water jars, the kind used by the Jews for ceremonial washing, each holding from twenty to thirty gallons.

[7] Jesus said to the servants, "Fill the jars with water"; so they filled them to the brim.

[8] Then he told them, "Now draw some out and take it to the master of the banquet."

They did so, [9] and the master of the banquet tasted the water that had been turned into wine. He did not realise where it had come from, though the servants who had drawn the water knew. Then he called the bridegroom aside [10] and said, "Everyone brings out the choice wine first and then the cheaper wine after the guests have had too much to drink; but you have saved the best till now."

Weddings

Weddings lasted for days in Jesus' time with the guests becoming more and more legless as the feast progressed - they brought out the vin de Tesco when people were too drunk to care! **Ephesians Ch 5 v18** tells us...

"Do not get drunk on wine which leads to debauchery [wild living]. Instead, be filled with the Spirit". Literally "be continually being filled."

[11] This, the first of his miraculous signs, Jesus performed at Cana in Galilee. He thus revealed his glory, and his disciples put their faith in him.

No more Mr Nice Guy!!!

[12] After this he went down to Capernaum with his mother and brothers and his disciples. There they stayed for a few days. (Passover see page 29)

[13] When it was almost time for the Jewish Passover, Jesus went up to Jerusalem. [14] In the temple courts he found men selling cattle, sheep and doves, and others sitting at tables exchanging money. [15] So he made a whip out of cords, and drove all from the temple area, both sheep and cattle; he scattered the coins of the money-changers and overturned their tables. [16] To those who sold doves he said, "Get these out of here! How dare you turn my Father's house into a market!"

[17] His disciples remembered that it is written: "Zeal for your house will consume me."

[18] Then the Jews demanded of him, "What miraculous sign can you show us to prove your authority to do all this?"

[19] Jesus answered them, "Destroy this temple, and I will raise it again in three days."

[20] The Jews replied, "It has taken forty-six years to build this temple, and you are going to raise it in three days?" [21] But the temple he had spoken of was his body. [22] After he was raised from the dead, his disciples recalled what he had said. Then they believed the Scripture and the words that Jesus had spoken.

whip!!?

Jesus is not a party pooper! He replaces the fleeting pleasure of drunkenness with the excitement and joy of the Holy Spirit.

This statement was to get Jesus into a lot of trouble! See Matthew Ch 26 vv60-62.

*Many people were drawn to Jesus by the sensational stuff he did, **but had no intention of having their hearts and attitudes changed!***

[23] Now while he was in Jerusalem at the Passover Feast, many people saw the miraculous signs he was doing and believed in his name. [24] But Jesus would not entrust himself to them, for he knew all men. [25] He did not need man's testimony about man, for he knew what was in a man.

Jesus was not looking for peoples' approval, his approval came from God the Father.

chapter

Now there was a man of the Pharisees named Nicodemus, a member of the Jewish ruling council. [2] He came to Jesus at night and said, "Rabbi, we know you are a teacher who has come from God. For no-one could perform the miraculous signs you are doing if God were not with him."

[3] In reply Jesus declared, "I tell you the truth, no-one can see the kingdom of God unless he is born again."

*The Bible says that I am 'dead in my sin' (See Ephesians Ch2 v1) before I hand over my life to Jesus. Obviously my body is alive, but my spirit is dead. The spirit is the bit of us humans which is able to **plug into God**.*

[4] "How can a man be born when he is old?" Nicodemus asked. "Surely he cannot enter a second time into his mother's womb to be born!"

[5] Jesus answered, "I tell you the truth, no-one can enter the kingdom of God unless he is born of water and the Spirit. [6] Flesh gives birth to flesh, but the Spirit gives birth to spirit. [7] You should not be surprised at my saying, 'You must be born again.' [8] The wind blows wherever it pleases. You hear its sound, but you cannot tell where it comes from or where it is going. So it is with everyone born of the Spirit."

Q. How can I have a relationship with God who is Spirit if my spirit is dead?

A. I need to be born again.

[9] "How can this be?" Nicodemus asked.

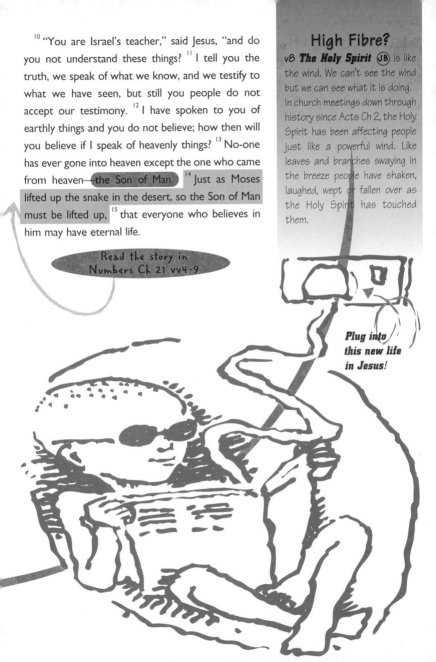

¹⁰ "You are Israel's teacher," said Jesus, "and do you not understand these things? ¹¹ I tell you the truth, we speak of what we know, and we testify to what we have seen, but still you people do not accept our testimony. ¹² I have spoken to you of earthly things and you do not believe; how then will you believe if I speak of heavenly things? ¹³ No-one has ever gone into heaven except the one who came from heaven—the Son of Man. ¹⁴ Just as Moses lifted up the snake in the desert, so the Son of Man must be lifted up, ¹⁵ that everyone who believes in him may have eternal life.

Read the story in Numbers Ch 21 vv4-9

High Fibre?

v8 **The Holy Spirit** (JB) is like the wind. We can't see the wind but we can see what it is doing. In church meetings down through history since Acts Ch 2, the Holy Spirit has been affecting people just like a powerful wind. Like leaves and branches swaying in the breeze people have shaken, laughed, wept or fallen over as the Holy Spirit has touched them.

Plug into this new life in Jesus!

serious
Lurv...

Perish: speaks of spiritual death or separation from God, for ever!

Because of our sin, we are separated from God already and under sentence of death (Romans Ch 6 v23 *"the wages of sin is death"*). The verdict has aready been given, we are condemned already! (v18)

But.... God loves us so much that he provided a way to declare us "not guilty"! It was to lay the guilt on Jesus - who had never sinned - and punish him instead of us

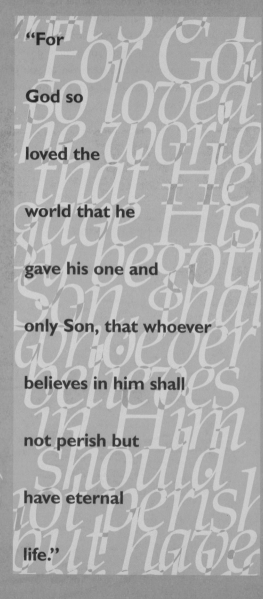

Jesus took the full force of God's anger against sin, dying the slow, cruel death of Roman crucifixion so we could get off scot free!!

We now have a choice: to accept Jesus and what he has done for us and go free, or to reject him and face the consequences...??

"For

God so

loved the

world that he

gave his one and

only Son, that whoever

believes in him shall

not perish but

have eternal

life."

[16] "For God so loved the world that he gave his one and only Son, that whoever believes in him shall not perish but have eternal life. [17] For God did not send his Son into the world to condemn the world, but to save the world through him. [18] Whoever believes in him is not condemned, but whoever does not believe stands condemned already because he has not believed in the name of God's one and only Son. [19] This is the verdict: Light has come into the world, but men loved darkness instead of light because their deeds were evil. [20] Everyone who does evil hates the light, and will not come into the light for fear that his deeds will be exposed. [21] But whoever lives by the truth comes into the light, so that it may be seen plainly that what he has done has been done through God."

[22] After this, Jesus and his disciples went out into the Judean countryside, where he spent some time with them, and baptised. [23] Now John also was baptising at Aenon near Salim, because there was plenty of water, and people were constantly coming to be baptised. [24] (This was before John was put in prison.) [25] An argument developed between some of John's disciples and a certain Jew over the matter of ceremonial washing. [26] They came to John and said to him, "Rabbi, that man who was with you on the other side of the Jordan—the one you testified about—well, he is baptising, and everyone is going to him."

[27] To this John replied, "A man can receive only what is given him from heaven. [28] You yourselves can testify that I said, 'I am not the Christ but am sent ahead of him.' [29] The (bride) belongs to the bridegroom. The friend who attends the (bridegroom)

Those who really want to live by the truth will be attracted to Jesus like a moth is to a light.

John was sent by God, but couldn't go beyond what God had given him to do. He knew what he wasn't!

John "T" Bap knew that he must fade out of the picture to let Jesus take centre stage. He knew that Jesus had come from heaven, whilst he was from the earth.

waits and listens for him, and is full of joy when he hears the bridegroom's voice. That joy is mine, and it is now complete. [30] He must become greater; I must become less.

[31] "The one who comes from above is above all; the one who is from the earth belongs to the earth, and speaks as one from the earth. The one who comes from heaven is above all. [32] He testifies to what he has seen and heard, but no-one accepts his testimony. [33] The man who has accepted it has certified that God is truthful. [34] For the one whom God has sent speaks the words of God, for God gives the Spirit without limit. [35] The Father loves the Son and has placed everything in his hands. [36] Whoever believes in the Son has eternal life, but whoever rejects the Son will not see life, for God's wrath remains on him."

Eternal Life

is not so much about how long we will live, as about the quality of life. Eternal life is the kind of life enjoyed in heaven, in God's undiluted presence.

We begin that amazing life when we are born again! The joy and peace we begin to experience are tasters of heaven. (Someone said "eternal life is not pie in the sky when you die, but cake on the plate while you wait!" - Catch the drift??)

Jesus talks with a... Samaritan woman!

chapter 4

Oi!!

The Pharisees heard that Jesus was gaining and baptising more disciples than John, [2] although in fact it was not Jesus who baptised, but his disciples. [3] When the Lord learned of this, he left Judea and went back once more to Galilee.

[4] Now he had to go through Samaria. [5] So he came to a town in Samaria called Sychar, near the plot of ground Jacob had given to his son Joseph. [6] Jacob's well was there, and Jesus, tired as he was from the journey, sat down by the well. It was about the sixth hour. ← *Midday, well hot!*

[7] When a Samaritan woman came to draw water, Jesus said to her, "Will you give me a drink?" [8] (His disciples had gone into the town to buy food.)

[9] The Samaritan woman said to him, "You are a Jew and I am a Samaritan woman. How can you ask me for a drink?" (For Jews do not associate with Samaritans.)

[10] Jesus answered her, "If you knew the gift of God and who it is that asks you for a drink, you would have asked him and he would have given you living water." ← *See notes at Ch 7 v33*

[11] "Sir," the woman said, "you have nothing to draw with and the well is deep. Where can you get this living water? [12] Are you greater than our father Jacob, who gave us the well and drank from it himself, as did also his sons and his flocks and herds?"

[13] Jesus answered, "Everyone who drinks this

High Fibre?

Samaritans: The Jews were seriously **racially prejudiced** towards the Samaritans. Samaria had originally been the Northern Kingdom of the Israelite nation. In 722 B.C., it was conquered by the Assyrians. (Who liked their lager and football... get the picture?!) They took off anyone who could work as slaves, leaving the dodgy looking ones to tend the land.

Foreigners moved into the land and the locals married some of them. Thus they lost their "ethnic purity", much to the disgust of their relatives next door.

Any self-respecting Jew would take a long detour rather than go through Samaria.

Jesus totally cut through the prejudices - he not only spoke with a woman which was bad enough!, but she was a Samaritan woman!! (Serious no-no for high flying religious types)

God's love does not "see" racial boundaries or social class. Phew!!

*Jesus and the woman were having two separate conversations!
The woman was talking about the natural world, Jesus was talking about the spiritual world. **Watch out for this.**

Jesus could only have known this by supernatural means!

The Samaritans had closed their minds to the writings of the O.T. prophets - they only had the first five books of the Bible, (known as the Pentateuch).

High Fibre?

Jesus was pointing to the **New Era** he was bringing, when the **real business** would be in the spirits of men and women, not in religious ceremonies or on holy mountains. This was prophesied by Jeremiah in the O.T. book named after him **Ch 31 w33-34.**

water will be thirsty again, ¹⁴ but whoever drinks the water I give him will never thirst. Indeed, the water I give him will become in him a spring of water welling up to eternal life."

¹⁵ The woman said to him, "Sir, give me this water so that I won't get thirsty and have to keep coming here to draw water."

¹⁶ He told her, "Go, call your husband and come back."

¹⁷ "I have no husband," she replied.

Jesus said to her, "You are right when you say you have no husband. ¹⁸ The fact is, you have had five husbands, and the man you now have is not your husband. What you have just said is quite true."

¹⁹ "Sir," the woman said, "I can see that you are a prophet. ²⁰ Our fathers worshipped on this mountain, but you Jews claim that the place where we must worship is in Jerusalem."

²¹ Jesus declared, "Believe me, woman, a time is coming when you will worship the Father neither on this mountain nor in Jerusalem. ²² You Samaritans worship what you do not know; we worship what we do know, for salvation is from the Jews. ²³ Yet a time is coming and has now come when the true worshippers will worship the Father in spirit and truth, for they are the kind of worshippers the Father seeks. ²⁴ God is spirit, and his worshippers must worship in spirit and in truth."

²⁵ The woman said, "I know that Messiah" (called Christ) "is coming. When he comes, he will explain everything to us."

²⁶ Then Jesus declared, "I who speak to you am he."

This is the only time Jesus openly said that he was the **Messiah** before his trial. Jesus gave great treasures to the outcasts of society - he is still the same today!!

²⁷ Just then his disciples returned and were surprised to find him talking with a woman. But no-one asked, "What do you want?" or "Why are you talking with her?"

Feel that prejudice towards the Samaritan woman!

²⁸ Then, leaving her water jar, the woman went back to the town and said to the people, ²⁹ "Come, see a man who told me everything I ever did. Could this be the Christ?" ³⁰ They came out of the town and made their way towards him.

³¹ Meanwhile his disciples urged him, "Rabbi, eat something."

³² But he said to them, "I have food to eat that you know nothing about."

There is a great **buzz** about telling people about God's love. It can be more satisfying than a good meal!

³³ Then his disciples said to each other, "Could someone have brought him food?"

³⁴ "My food," said Jesus, "is to do the will of him who sent me and to finish his work. ³⁵Do you not say, 'Four months more and then the harvest'? I tell you, open your eyes and look at the fields! They are ripe for harvest. ³⁶ Even now the reaper draws his wages, even now he harvests the crop for eternal life, so that the sower and the reaper may be glad together. ³⁷ Thus the saying 'One sows and another reaps' is true. ³⁸ I sent you to reap what you have not worked for. Others have done the hard work, and you have reaped the benefits of their labour."

Jesus words to the woman at the well started a ripple effect in the area. People just had to come and meet Jesus for themselves. **Something pretty radical must have taken place in that woman's life!**

³⁹ Many of the Samaritans from that town believed in him because of the woman's testimony, "He told me everything I ever did." ⁴⁰ So when the Samaritans came to him, they urged him to stay with them, and he stayed two days. ⁴¹ And because of his words many more became believers.

⁴² They said to the woman, "We no longer believe just because of what you said; now we have

If God has touched your life, give it away! Tell other people about it and let them enjoy what you have found!

heard for ourselves, and we know that this man really is the (Saviour) of the world."

⁴³ After the two days he left for Galilee. ⁴⁴ (Now Jesus himself had pointed out that a prophet has no honour in his own country.) ⁴⁵ When he arrived in Galilee, the Galileans welcomed him. They had seen all that he had done in Jerusalem at the Passover Feast, for they also had been there.

⁴⁶ Once more he visited Cana in Galilee, where he had turned the water into wine. And there was a certain royal official whose son lay sick at Capernaum. ⁴⁷ When this man heard that Jesus had arrived in Galilee from Judea, he went to him and begged him to come and heal his son, who was close to death.

⁴⁸ "Unless you people see miraculous signs and wonders," Jesus told him, "you will never believe."

⁴⁹ The royal official said, "Sir, come down before my child dies."

⁵⁰ Jesus replied, "You may go. Your son will live." The man took Jesus at his word and departed.

⁵¹ While he was still on the way, his servants met him with the news that his boy was living. ⁵² When he enquired as to the time when his son got better, they said to him, "The fever left him yesterday at the seventh hour."

⁵³ Then the father realised that this was the exact time at which Jesus had said to him, "Your son will live." So he and all his household believed.

⁵⁴ This was the second miraculous sign that Jesus performed, having come from Judea to Galilee.

Jesus is the **Word of God**, (remember Chapter 1). He speaks and awesome things happen! YES!

The pool of Bethesda seems to have had some mystical healing powers. When the waters began to bubble all the sick people took a dive for the water. Only the first to get in would be healed. ...Last one in's a dummy!

The paralysed guy had a bit of a disadvantage!

5

Some time later, Jesus went up to Jerusalem for a feast of the Jews. ² Now there is in Jerusalem near the Sheep Gate a pool, which in Aramaic is called Bethesda and which is surrounded by five covered colonnades. ³ Here a great number of disabled people used to lie—the blind, the lame, the paralysed. ⁵One who was there had been an invalid for thirty-eight years. ⁶ When Jesus saw him lying there and learned that he had been in this condition for a long time, he asked him, ("Do you want to get well?")

⁷ "Sir," the invalid replied, "I have no-one to help me into the pool when the water is stirred. While I am trying to get in, someone else goes down ahead of me."

⁸ Then Jesus said to him, "Get up! Pick up your mat and walk." ⁹ At once the man was cured; he picked up his mat and walked.

The day on which this took place was a Sabbath, ¹⁰ and so the Jews said to the man who had been healed, "It is the Sabbath; the law forbids you to carry your mat."

¹¹But he replied, "The man who made me well said to me, 'Pick up your mat and walk.' "

¹² So they asked him, "Who is this fellow who told you to pick it up and walk?"

¹³ The man who was healed had no idea who it

High Fibre?

Sabbath: In the **Ten Commandments** God set apart the Sabbath, (our Saturday) as a day of rest. God's plan was that people should have time to spend with him and with their families - not working non-stop, seven days a week.

The Pharisees and religious boffs were far more bothered that Jesus had "worked" on the Sabbath than that one poor paralysed beggar had been amazingly healed!

Stupid question?... No! Some beggars were professionals and might not want to lose their source of income.

Do you want to change???? Are you happy to stay dead, not knowing God's amazing love, or will you let Jesus touch your life and change it for ever?

was, for Jesus had slipped away into the crowd that was there.

¹⁴ Later Jesus found him at the temple and said to him, "See, you are well again. Stop sinning or something worse may happen to you." ¹⁵ The man went away and told the Jews that it was Jesus who had made him well.

¹⁶ So, because Jesus was doing these things on the Sabbath, the Jews persecuted him. ¹⁷ Jesus said to them, "My Father is always at his work to this very day, and I, too, am working." ¹⁸ For this reason the Jews tried all the harder to kill him; not only was he breaking the Sabbath, but he was even calling God his own Father, making himself equal with God.

¹⁹ Jesus gave them this answer: "I tell you the truth, the Son can do nothing by himself; he can do only what he sees his Father doing, because whatever the Father does the Son also does. ²⁰ For the Father loves the Son and shows him all he does. Yes, to your amazement he will show him even greater things than these. ²¹ For just as the Father raises the dead and gives them life, even so the Son gives life to whom he is pleased to give it. ²² Moreover, the Father judges no-one, but has entrusted all judgment to the Son, ²³ that all may honour the Son just as they honour the Father. He who does not honour the Son does not honour the Father, who sent him.

²⁴ "I tell you the truth, whoever hears my word and believes him who sent me has eternal life and will not be condemned; he has crossed over from death to life. ²⁵ I tell you the truth, a time is coming and has now come when the dead will hear the voice of the Son of God and those who hear will live. ²⁶ For as the Father has life in himself, so he has granted the

Sin JB: was the deeper problem in the man's life - it can destroy for ever!

If Jesus was not who he claimed to be... then he was a con-man and a liar!

One God

People struggle to understand how **Jesus, the Father and the Holy Spirit can be one God.** They are in total harmony together, each honouring the other.

They are totally one in heart and mind and are equally God, yet have different jobs to do. My body, soul and spirit are all me, but have different functions.

v19: Jesus never acted independently from the Father. He demonstrates the really close relationship God wants us to have with him.

Son to have life in himself. [27] And he has given him authority to judge because he is the Son of Man.

[28] "Do not be amazed at this, for a time is coming when all who are in their graves will hear his voice [29] and come out—those who have done good will rise to live, and those who have done evil will rise to be condemned. [30] By myself I can do nothing; I judge only as I hear, and my judgment is just, (for I seek not to please myself but him who sent me.)

[31] "If I testify about myself, my testimony is not valid. [32] There is another who testifies in my favour, and I know that his testimony about me is valid.

[33] "You have sent to John and he has testified to the truth. [34] Not that I accept human testimony; but I mention it that you may be saved. [35] John was a lamp that burned and gave light, and you chose for a time to enjoy his light.

[36] "I have testimony weightier than that of John. For the very work that the Father has given me to finish, and which I am doing, testifies that the Father has sent me. [37] And the Father who sent me has himself testified concerning me. You have never heard his voice nor seen his form, [38] nor does his word dwell in you, for you do not believe the one he sent. [39] You diligently study the Scriptures because you think that by them you possess eternal life. These are the Scriptures that testify about me, [40] yet you refuse to come to me to have life.

Only the creator God has life in himself. Jesus is God. (See John Ch 1 v1)

Although Jesus said this He is our perfect example of how to live a life which pleases the Father.

The Christian no longer lives to please him/herself, but God.

Old Testament

Prophecy - the writings of Moses, plus the prophetic writings and the Psalms all contain prophetic bits which Jesus fulfilled. Many are odd little verses here and there which are easily missed. It is absolutely amazing how accurate these prophecies are.

Isaiah wrote 700 years B.C. about how the Messiah would suffer. Jesus only happened to be born in Bethlehem because of a crazy Roman Census - yet **Micah** wrote around the same time as Isaiah that Jesus would be from Bethlehem! Hosea wrote in the 750-725 B.C. slot: "Out of Egypt I called my son" Hozea Ch 11 v1 . It just happened that Mary and Joseph took baby Jesus to Egypt to escape the hostile interest of King Herod.

⁴¹ "I do not accept praise from men, ⁴² but I know you. I know that you do not have the love of God in your hearts. ⁴³ I have come in my Father's name, and you do not accept me; but if someone else comes in his own name, you will accept him. ⁴⁴ How can you believe if you accept praise from one another, yet make no effort to obtain the praise that comes from the only God?

⁴⁵ "But do not think I will accuse you before the Father. Your accuser is Moses, on whom your hopes are set. ⁴⁶ If you believed Moses, you would believe me, for he wrote about me. ⁴⁷ But since you do not believe what he wrote, how are you going to believe what I say?"

Moses foretold Jesus' coming in the O.T. book of Deuteronomy Ch 18 vv15-19.

oh boy! it's question time

Great! I was just enjoying the sermon!

TORPEDO ROLL

Jesus x 5,000
FEEDS THE

Ch6
Some time after this, Jesus crossed to the far shore of the Sea of Galilee (that is, the Sea of Tiberias), ²and a great crowd of people followed him because they saw the miraculous signs he had performed on the sick. ³Then Jesus went up on a mountainside and sat down with his disciples. ⁴ The Jewish Passover Feast was near.

The reason why there were so many people around.

⁵ When Jesus looked up and saw a great crowd coming towards him, he said to Philip, "Where shall we buy bread for these people to eat?" ⁶ He asked this only to test him, for he already had in mind what he was going to do.

Jesus had already been in touch with H.Q.!

⁷ Philip answered him, "Eight months' wages would not buy enough bread for each one to have a bite!"

⁸ Another of his disciples, Andrew, Simon Peter's brother, spoke up, ⁹ "Here is a boy with five small barley loaves and two small fish, but how far will they go among so many?"

¹⁰ Jesus said, "Make the people sit down." There was plenty of grass in that place, and the men sat down, about five thousand of them. ¹¹ Jesus then took the loaves, gave thanks, and distributed to those who were seated as much as they wanted. He did the same with the fish.

¹² When they had all had enough to eat, he said to his disciples, "Gather the pieces that are left over. Let nothing be wasted." ¹³ So they gathered them and filled twelve baskets with the pieces of the five barley loaves left over by those who had eaten.

¹⁴ After the people saw the miraculous sign that Jesus did, they began to say, "Surely this is the Prophet who is to come into the world." ¹⁵ Jesus, knowing that they intended to come and make him king by force, withdrew again to a mountain by himself.

High Fibre?

Man - na - live! The people were well hung-up about the idea that Jesus was the Prophet that Moses spoke about. Because of that they thought he should do the things Moses did. When Moses led the Israelites in the desert they ate bread from heaven called manna.

(See Numbers Ch11 v7-9).

Jesus is a keen environmentalist - maybe he wore green wellies and not sandals after all?

God is not stingy!!

Jesus walks... on the water!

WARNING - we advise you not to try this at home!

¹⁶ When evening came, his disciples went down to the lake, ¹⁷ where they got into a boat and set off across the lake for Capernaum. By now it was dark, and Jesus had not yet joined them. ¹⁸ A strong wind

Jesus defies the laws of nature – he made them in the first place!

The going can be extremely tough, but it sure gets easier when Jesus is in the boat.

was blowing and the waters grew rough. [19] When they had rowed three or three and a half miles, they saw Jesus approaching the boat, walking on the water; and they were terrified. [20] But he said to them, "It is I; don't be afraid." [21] Then they were willing to take him into the boat, and immediately the boat reached the shore where they were heading.

[22] The next day the crowd that had stayed on the opposite shore of the lake realised that only one boat had been there, and that Jesus had not entered it with his disciples, but that they had gone away alone. [23] Then some boats from Tiberias landed near the place where the people had eaten the bread after the Lord had given thanks. [24] Once the crowd realised that neither Jesus nor his disciples were there, they got into the boats and went to Capernaum in search of Jesus.

[25] When they found him on the other side of the lake, they asked him, "Rabbi, when did you get here?"

[26] Jesus answered, "I tell you the truth, you are looking for me, not because you saw miraculous

Who's who in the... Bible

Chief Priests - these were the descendants of Aaron, Moses' brother. They would include that year's High Priest, plus all the big shots in the priest dept. Many would also have been members of the Sanhedrin, the Jewish parliament allowed by the Romans.

The Jews - is a phrase John uses many times to lump together the Orthodox Jews who dissagreed with Jesus.

Pharisees (JB) - were an exclusive religious sect. They were highly legalistic, trying to follow every tiny bit of the Law. Jesus mercilessly exposed their hypocrisy as they claimed to be so perfect yet missed the target by a million miles! **They added** to God's Word lots of additional laws which God had never set.

Sadduccees - these took away from God's word. They were cynical, not believing in anything too supernatural such as angels and demons. They did not believe in life after death. They were a more secular group - upper-middle class and politically influential.

signs but because you ate the loaves and had your fill. ²⁷ Do not work for food that spoils, but for food that endures to eternal life, which the Son of Man will give you. On him God the Father has placed his seal of approval."

²⁸ Then they asked him, "What must we do to do the works God requires?"

²⁹ Jesus answered, "The work of God is this: to believe in the one he has sent."

³⁰ So they asked him, "What miraculous sign then will you give that we may see it and believe you? What will you do? ³¹ Our forefathers ate the manna in the desert; as it is written: 'He gave them bread from heaven to eat.'"

³² Jesus said to them, "I tell you the truth, it is not Moses who has given you the bread from heaven, but it is my Father who gives you the true bread from heaven. ³³ For the bread of God is he who comes down from heaven and gives life to the world."

³⁴ "Sir," they said, "from now on give us this bread."

³⁵ Then Jesus declared, "I am the bread of life. He who comes to me will never go hungry, and he who believes in me will never be thirsty. ³⁶ But as I told you, you have seen me and still you do not believe. ³⁷ All that the Father gives me will come to me, and whoever comes to me I will never drive away. ³⁸ For I have come down from heaven not to do my will but to do the will of him who sent me. ³⁹ And this is the will of him who sent me, that I shall lose none of all that he has given me, but raise them up at the last day. ⁴⁰ For my Father's will is that everyone who looks to the Son and believes in him shall have eternal life, and I will raise him up at the last day." • • • • • • • •

> The work which really pleases God is believing in Jesus.

High Fibre?

Jesus says "Hey guys, don't you realise the manna was just a symbol of me - the bread of life?" Jesus came from heaven to satisfy the spiritual hunger of mankind: the need for relationship with God.

Verses 37-40
JAM HOT
Yes Sir-ree !!

See notes on resurrection in the JARGONBUSTER

Those who are really listening to God will find Jesus.

Wind-up session!!

Jesus knew that many people were following him for the wrong reasons - like they enjoyed the free lunches and watching the occasional miracle! He knew that the very thought of eating human flesh was enough to get a nice religious Pharisee into a sweat!

The law was very strict about what kind of meat you could eat - human was definitely off the menu!

(Actually Jesus was talking in pictures again.)

High Fibre?

Contrary to some popular belief, Jesus was not saying that the bread and wine used in **Holy Communion** actually become his flesh and blood! (Yuk!)

God has never given the O.K. to cannibalism!

Jesus was actually talking more along the lines of his life being a sacrifice for the sin of the whole world, as in **John Ch 1 v29.**

⁴¹ At this the Jews began to grumble about him because he said, "I am the bread that came down from heaven." ⁴² They said, "Is this not Jesus, the son of Joseph, whose father and mother we know? How can he now say, 'I came down from heaven'?"

⁴³ "Stop grumbling among yourselves," Jesus answered. ⁴⁴ "No-one can come to me unless the Father who sent me draws him, and I will raise him up at the last day. ⁴⁵ It is written in the Prophets: 'They will all be taught by God.' Everyone who listens to the Father and learns from him comes to me. ⁴⁶ No-one has seen the Father except the one who is from God; only he has seen the Father. ⁴⁷ I tell you the truth, he who believes has everlasting life. ⁴⁸ I am the bread of life. ⁴⁹ Your forefathers ate the manna in the desert, yet they died. ⁵⁰ But here is the bread that comes down from heaven, which a man may eat and not die. ⁵¹ I am the living bread that came down from heaven. If anyone eats of this bread, he will live for ever. This bread is my flesh, which I will give for the life of the world."

⁵² Then the Jews began to argue sharply among themselves, "How can this man give us his flesh to eat?"

⁵³ Jesus said to them, "I tell you the truth, unless you eat the flesh of the Son of Man and drink his blood, you have no life in you. ⁵⁴ Whoever eats my flesh and drinks my blood has eternal life, and I will raise him up at the last day. ⁵⁵ For my flesh is real food and my blood is real drink. ⁵⁶ Whoever eats my flesh and drinks my blood remains in me, and I in him. ⁵⁷ Just as the living Father sent me and

I live because of the Father, so the one who feeds on me will live because of me. [58] This is the bread that came down from heaven. Your forefathers ate manna and died, but he who feeds on this bread will live for ever." [59] He said this while teaching in the synagogue in Capernaum.

DO NOT READ THIS

The Passover

A lamb was killed for the Passover meal as a kind of sacrifice. (**Read Exodus 12 in the O.T.**). After some of its blood had been daubed on the doorposts of the house, the lamb was roasted and eaten by the family. This ceremony shows us some things about Jesus' sacrifice:

1. The animal was well dead. It was roasted and eaten! Jesus had to really die. (Not just faint on the cross and then revive in the cool of the tomb!)

2. The person eating was responsible. All who ate the lamb had agreed with its death. I must make Jesus' death count for me personally; not just believe in a vague, general kind of way.

3. The eaters received a benefit. They were all protected from God's judgment, plus they had a slap-up roast dinner to celebrate!

Because of Jesus' death for me, I escape God's judgement, while receiving many benefits in this life through what Jesus has done.

Drinking blood under O.T. law was totally forbidden. God said " the life of a creature is in the blood"
   (Leviticus Ch 17 v11 in the O.T.).

Jesus was saying that the life that was in him, I need in me.

[60] On hearing it, many of his disciples said, "This is a hard teaching. Who can accept it?"

[61] Aware that his disciples were grumbling about this, Jesus said to them, "Does this offend you? [62] What if you see the Son of Man ascend to where he was before! [63] The Spirit gives life; the flesh counts for nothing. The words I have spoken to you are spirit and they are life. [64] Yet there are some of you who do not believe." For Jesus had known from the

beginning which of them did not believe and who would betray him. [65] He went on to say, "This is why I told you that no-one can come to me unless the Father has enabled him." [66] From this time many of his disciples turned back and no longer followed him.

[67] "You do not want to leave too, do you?" Jesus asked the Twelve.

[68] Simon Peter answered him, "Lord, to whom shall we go? You have the words of eternal life. [69] We believe and know that you are the Holy One of God."

[70] Then Jesus replied, "Have I not chosen you, the Twelve? Yet one of you is a devil!" [71] (He meant Judas, the son of Simon Iscariot, who, though one of the Twelve, was later to betray him.)

However much the twelve disciples struggled with some of the things Jesus said, they knew they must stay with him because he had what they needed – **Life!**

Jesus was not caught by surprise by Judas – he chose him on purpose. He also loved him and treated him the same as all the others.

THE feast of TABERNACLES

Chapter 7 After this, Jesus went around in Galilee, purposely staying away from Judea because the Jews there were waiting to take his life. [2] But when the Jewish Feast of Tabernacles was near, [3] Jesus' brothers said to him, "You ought to leave here and go to Judea, so that your disciples may see the miracles you do. [4] No-one who wants to become a public figure acts in secret. Since you are doing these things, show yourself to

The Feast of Tabernacles

To celebrate the harvest and to remember the time when the Israelites lived in tents, during the feast of tabernacles everyone made little tents from leafy branches.
They had a week off work, lived in their little leafy tent (or **tabernacle**) and got down to some serious feasting!
Great fun and relaxation!

the world." [5] For even his own brothers did not believe in him.

[6] Therefore Jesus told them, ("The right time for me has not yet come; for you any time is right.") [7] The world cannot hate you, but it hates me because I testify that what it does is evil. [8] You go to the Feast. I am not yet going up to this Feast, because for me the right time has not yet come." [9] Having said this, he stayed in Galilee.

[10] However, after his brothers had left for the Feast, he went also, not publicly, but in secret. [11] Now at the Feast the Jews were watching for him and asking, "Where is that man?"

[12] Among the crowds there was widespread whispering about him. Some said, "He is a good man."

Others replied, "No, he deceives the people." [13] But no-one would say anything publicly about him for fear of the Jews.

[14] Not until halfway through the Feast did Jesus go up to the temple courts and begin to teach. [15] The Jews were amazed and asked, ("How did this man get such learning without having studied?")

[16] Jesus answered, "My teaching is not my own. It comes from him who sent me. [17] If anyone chooses to do God's will, he will find out whether my teaching comes from God or whether I speak on my own. [18] He who speaks on his own does so to gain honour for himself, but he who works for the honour of the one who sent him is a man of truth; there is nothing false about him. [19] Has not Moses given you the law? Yet not one of you keeps the law. Why are you trying to kill me?"

[20] "You are demon-possessed," the crowd answered. "Who is trying to kill you?"

Jesus's life was not a series of random events, but a perfectly timed mission.

Jesus had a great teacher!

Anyone who really wants to please God will know that Jesus is from God.

High-pitched Fibre?

Circumcision: **JB** Jewish boys were circumcised (**oooooch!!**) on their eighth day, whatever day of the week that happened to be. The religious boffs were very happy to work on the Sabbath by circumcising someone's little boy, but got very sniffy **about Jesus healing on the Sabbath!** Hmm!

Circumcision was an O.T. requirement given as an **external sign** that the Jews belonged to God. (It was also probably quite hygienic!) **However, it is our heart's attitude which really shows the world that we belong to God.**

God often got angry with Israel for being circumcised outwardly but full of sin inside.

(Note: The circumcision deal is off since Jesus came!)

²¹ Jesus said to them, "I did one miracle, and you are all astonished. ²² Yet, because Moses gave you circumcision (though actually it did not come from Moses, but from the patriarchs), you circumcise a child on the Sabbath. ²³ Now if a child can be circumcised on the Sabbath so that the law of Moses may not be broken, why are you angry with me for healing the whole man on the Sabbath? ²⁴ Stop judging by mere appearances, and make a right judgment."

²⁵ At that point some of the people of Jerusalem began to ask, "Isn't this the man they are trying to kill? ²⁶ Here he is, speaking publicly, and they are not saying a word to him. Have the authorities really concluded that he is the Christ? ²⁷ But we know where this man is from; when the Christ comes, no-one will know where he is from."

²⁸ Then Jesus, still teaching in the temple courts, cried out, "Yes, you know me, and you know where I am from. I am not here on my own, but he who sent me is true. You do not know him, ²⁹ but I know him because I am from him and he sent me."

³⁰ At this they tried to seize him, but no-one laid a hand on him, because his time had not yet come. ³¹ Still, many in the crowd put their faith in him. They said, "When the Christ comes, will he do more miraculous signs than this man?"

³² The Pharisees heard the crowd whispering such things about him. Then the chief priests and the Pharisees sent temple guards to arrest him.

³³ Jesus said, "I am with you for only a short time, and then I go to the one who sent me. ³⁴ You will

look for me, but you will not find me; and where I am, you cannot come."

[35] The Jews said to one another, "Where does this man intend to go that we cannot find him? Will he go where our people live scattered among the Greeks, and teach the Greeks? [36] What did he mean when he said, 'You will look for me, but you will not find me,' and 'Where I am, you cannot come'?"

[37] On the last and greatest day of the Feast, Jesus stood and said in a loud voice, "If anyone is thirsty, let him come to me and drink. [38] Whoever believes in me, as the Scripture has said, streams of living water will flow from within him." [39] By this he meant the Spirit, whom those who believed in him were later to receive. Up to that time the Spirit had not been given, since Jesus had not yet been glorified.

Living water

The people had been eating and drinking solidly for seven days at the point Jesus shouts "If anyone is still thirsty..."

However much we feed our natural appetites with food, sleep, sex or excitement, **we will always be** hungry underneath.

Only the Holy Spirit can really satisfy our inner thirst. He is like a continuously bubbling spring bringing the life of God up into our lives, fresh moment by moment.

(Read Acts 2 in the N.T. and see what happened .)

[40] On hearing his words, some of the people said, "Surely this man is the Prophet."

[41] Others said, "He is the Christ."

Still others asked, "How can the Christ come from Galilee? [42] Does not the Scripture say that the Christ will come from David's family and from Bethlehem, the town where David lived?" [43] Thus the people were divided because of Jesus. [44] Some

They obviously didn't realise that Jesus was actually born in Bethlehem.
Remember the Christmas story?

Even the guards were powerless before Jesus until the time set by God!.

That's true!

There never has been a religious leader, before or since who has spoken anything like Jesus! Around Jesus' time in history there were all kinds of people popping up claiming to be this or that... A bit like now!

Ch 7 v53–Ch 8 v11 (shown in orange) is a chunk of writing not found in the earliest copies of John's Gospel. Somehow it found it's way into the book, and has become a treasured story of Jesus' mercy and wisdom.

chapter 8

Jesus writing in the sand with his finger would have brought to the mind of the Pharisees, the Ten Commandments which God wrote with his own finger in slabs of stone. The finger of God is a symbol of great authority and of God's judgment!
See Daniel Ch 5 vv5,6

wanted to seize him, but no-one laid a hand on him.

[45] Finally the temple guards went back to the chief priests and Pharisees, who asked them, "Why didn't you bring him in?"

[46] "No-one ever spoke the way this man does," the guards declared.

[47] "You mean he has deceived you also?" the Pharisees retorted. [48] "Has any of the rulers or of the Pharisees believed in him? [49] No! But this mob that knows nothing of the law—there is a curse on them."

[50] Nicodemus, who had gone to Jesus earlier and who was one of their own number, asked, [51] "Does our law condemn a man without first hearing him to find out what he is doing?"

[52] They replied, "Are you from Galilee, too? Look into it, and you will find that a prophet does not come out of Galilee." [53] Then each went to his own home.

But Jesus went to the Mount of Olives. [2] At dawn he appeared again in the temple courts, where all the people gathered round him, and he sat down to teach them. [3] The teachers of the law and the Pharisees brought in a woman caught in adultery. They made her stand before the group [4] and said to Jesus, "Teacher, this woman was caught in the act of adultery. [5] In the Law Moses commanded us to stone such women. Now what do you say?" [6] They were using this question as a trap, in order to have a basis for accusing him.

But Jesus bent down and started to write on the ground with his finger. [7] When they kept on questioning him, he straightened up and said to them, "If any one of you is without sin, let him be the first to throw a stone at her." [8] Again he stooped down and wrote on the ground.

[9] At this, those who heard began to go away one at a time, the older ones first, until only Jesus was left, with the woman still standing there. [10] Jesus straightened up and asked her, "Woman, where are they? Has no-one condemned you?"

[11] "No-one, sir," she said.

"Then neither do I condemn you," Jesus declared. "Go now and leave your life of sin."

[12] When Jesus spoke again to the people, he said, "I am the light of the world. Whoever follows me will never walk in darkness, but will have the light of life."

[13] The Pharisees challenged him, "Here you are, appearing as your own witness; your testimony is not valid."

[14] Jesus answered, "Even if I testify on my own behalf, my testimony is valid, for I know where I came from and where I am going. But you have no idea where I come from or where I am going. [15] You judge by human standards; I pass judgment on no-one. [16] But if I do judge, my decisions are right, because I am not alone. I stand with the Father, who sent me. [17] In your own Law it is written that the testimony of two men is valid. [18] I am one who testifies for myself; my other witness is the Father, who sent me."

[19] Then they asked him, "Where is your father?"

"You do not know me or my Father," Jesus replied. "If you knew me, you would know my Father also." [20] He spoke these words while teaching in the temple area near the place where the offerings were put. Yet no-one seized him, because his time had not yet come.

Jesus totally floors them with his answer - "if any one of you is without sin,". He was showing mercy to the woman and saving her life while saying to to the crowd that sin is sin - no-one is innocent!

Notice Jesus did not say "It's o.k. love, carry on as you were!"

High Fibre?
Heavy Duty Hypocrisy!
Under O.T. law people caught in the act of committing adultery were stoned to death. However, the culprits had to be witnessed **(sounds like a job for a tabloid journalist!)**, and you had to catch them both. **(What happened to the guy eh?)** In bringing only the woman the **Pharisees (again!!)** were trying to trap Jesus. They wanted him to either get in trouble with the Romans who were not very happy about lynch mobs or with the O.T. law which clearly outlawed adultery.

The Jews were probably trying to make a snide remark about Jesus being an illegitimate child - Mary and Joseph were not married when he was conceived. ***Jesus ignores it and turns the tables on them in v41!***

A guy who has been going around raising the dead says to you "you will die in your sin" I would take a bit of notice!!

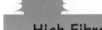

Jesus dropping hints about his forthcoming death on the cross.

High Fibre?

John Ch 14 v6 Jesus said "I am the way the truth and the life". If I live by Jesus' teaching I will begin to see the truth about myself and about God. I will be set free from the stranglehold of sin which leads to death and separation from God.

²¹ Once more Jesus said to them, "I am going away, and you will look for me, and you will die in your sin. Where I go, you cannot come."

²² This made the Jews ask, "Will he kill himself? Is that why he says, 'Where I go, you cannot come'?"

²³ But he continued, "You are from below; I am from above. You are of this world; I am not of this world. ²⁴ I told you that you would die in your sins; if you do not believe that I am ˪the one I claim to be˩, you will indeed die in your sins."

²⁵ "Who are you?" they asked.

"Just what I have been claiming all along," Jesus replied. ²⁶ "I have much to say in judgment of you. But he who sent me is reliable, and what I have heard from him I tell the world."

²⁷ They did not understand that he was telling them about his Father. ²⁸ So Jesus said, "When you have lifted up the Son of Man, then you will know that I am ˪the one I claim to be˩ and that I do nothing on my own but speak just what the Father has taught me. ²⁹ The one who sent me is with me; he has not left me alone, for I always do what pleases him." ³⁰ Even as he spoke, many put their faith in him.

³¹ To the Jews who had believed him, Jesus said, "If you hold to my teaching, you are really my disciples. ³² Then you will know the truth, and the truth will set you free."

³³ They answered him, "We are Abraham's descendants and have never been slaves of anyone. How can you say that we shall be set free?"

³⁴ Jesus replied, "I tell you the truth, everyone who sins is a slave to sin. ³⁵ Now a slave has no permanent place in the family, but a son belongs to it for ever. ³⁶ So if the Son sets you free, you will be free indeed.

[37] I know you are Abraham's descendants. Yet you are ready to kill me, because you have no room for my word. [38] I am telling you what I have seen in the Father's presence, and you do what you have heard from your father."

[39] "Abraham is our father," they answered.

"If you were Abraham's children," said Jesus, "then you would do the things Abraham did. [40] As it is, you are determined to kill me, a man who has told you the truth that I heard from God. Abraham did not do such things. [41] You are doing the things your own father does."

"We are not illegitimate children," they protested. "The only Father we have is God himself."

[42] Jesus said to them, "If God were your Father, you would love me, for I came from God and now am here. I have not come on my own; but he sent me. [43] Why is my language not clear to you? Because you are unable to hear what I say. [44] You belong to your father, the devil, and you want to carry out your father's desire. He was a murderer from the beginning, not holding to the truth, for there is no truth in him. When he lies, he speaks his native language, for he is a liar and the father of lies. [45] Yet

Jesus says clearly that **everyone is a slave to sin.** Sin is like a deadly cancer which everyone is born with.

> Only Jesus, (the Son) can set us free - by making us **"born-again"**.

Abraham believed in God even though he had very little to go on. **The Pharisees** had seen the amazing stuff Jesus had been doing, yet still refused to believe!

Low Fibre?

The Devil: The devil is not some mythical creature, he is an ex-angel called **Lucifer!** Angels are supernatural beings made by God to serve him. The Bible tells how the devil was a beautiful angel who rather fancied a go at being God! He soon found himself out of a job, along with a number of other angels who rebelled at the same time. (**Read O.T. book of** Isaiah Ch 14 w12-15)

He has a number of names - **Satan** (meaning, accuser), the **Evil One** and **Beelzebub.**

Jesus says that the **devil is the father of lies and a murderer.** He spends his time deceiving people.

> The lies of the devil always appeal to those who don't want to change, such as the Pharisees.

If the Jews could make everyone believe that Jesus was motivated by demonic forces they could ignore everything he said.

"I am" was the name God used when he revealed himself to Moses (Exodus Ch 3 v14). Jesus was using this name for himself - claiming to be the God of the O.T. - utter blasphemy as far as the Pharisees were concerned!

That's why they wanted to lynch him!

because I tell the truth, you do not believe me! ⁴⁶ Can any of you prove me guilty of sin? If I am telling the truth, why don't you believe me? ⁴⁷ He who belongs to God hears what God says. The reason you do not hear is that you do not belong to God."

⁴⁸ The Jews answered him, "Aren't we right in saying that you are a Samaritan and demon-possessed?"

⁴⁹ "I am not possessed by a demon," said Jesus, "but I honour my Father and you dishonour me. ⁵⁰ I am not seeking glory for myself; but there is one who seeks it, and he is the judge. ⁵¹ I tell you the truth, if anyone keeps my word, he will never see death."

⁵² At this the Jews exclaimed, "Now we know that you are demon-possessed! Abraham died and so did the prophets, yet you say that if anyone keeps your word, he will never taste death. ⁵³ Are you greater than our father Abraham? He died, and so did the prophets. Who do you think you are?"

⁵⁴ Jesus replied, "If I glorify myself, my glory means nothing. My Father, whom you claim as your God, is the one who glorifies me. ⁵⁵ Though you do not know him, I know him. If I said I did not, I would be a liar like you, but I do know him and keep his word. ⁵⁶ Your father Abraham rejoiced at the thought of seeing my day; he saw it and was glad."

⁵⁷ "You are not yet fifty years old," the Jews said to him, "and you have seen Abraham!"

⁵⁸ "I tell you the truth," Jesus answered, "before Abraham was born, I am!" ⁵⁹ At this, they picked up stones to stone him, but Jesus hid himself, slipping away from the temple grounds.

CHAPTER 9

As he went along, he saw a man blind from birth. 2 His disciples asked him, "Rabbi, who sinned, this man or his parents, that he was born blind?"

3 "Neither this man nor his parents sinned," said Jesus, "but this happened so that the work of God might be displayed in his life. 4 As long as it is day, we must do the work of him who sent me. Night is coming, when no-one can work. 5 While I am in the world, I am the light of the world."

6 Having said this, he spat on the ground, made some mud with the saliva, and put it on the man's eyes. 7 "Go," he told him, "wash in the Pool of Siloam" (this word means Sent). So the man went and washed, and came home seeing. **Yuk!**

8 His neighbours and those who had formerly seen him begging asked, "Isn't this the same man who used to sit and beg?" 9 Some claimed that he was.

Others said, "No, he only looks like him."

But he himself insisted, "I am the man."

10 "How then were your eyes opened?" they demanded.

11 He replied, "The man they call Jesus made some mud and put it on my eyes. He told me to go to Siloam and wash. So I went and washed, and then I could see."

12 "Where is this man?" they asked him.

"I don't know," he said.

13 They brought to the Pharisees the man who had been blind. 14 Now the day on which Jesus had made the mud and opened the man's eyes was a Sabbath.

WARNING

Don't assume that sickness or disability is a punishment from God. Jesus saw the man's blindness as an opportunity to demonstrate his love and power to the man.

We may not yet operate at the same level of healing power as Jesus, but we can still demonstrate his love to those who are sick or disabled. Pray for their healing too – you may be surprised!!

Verse 7 gave us a real "Wash and Go!"

Ooops too late! Spitting on the Sabbath! If you've not guessed it's a no-no.

[15] Therefore the Pharisees also asked him how he had received his sight. "He put mud on my eyes," the man replied, "and I washed, and now I see."

[16] Some of the Pharisees said, "This man is not from God, for he does not keep the Sabbath."

But others asked, "How can a sinner do such miraculous signs?" So they were divided.

[17] Finally they turned again to the blind man, "What have you to say about him? It was your eyes he opened."

The man replied, "He is a prophet."

[18] The Jews still did not believe that he had been blind and had received his sight until they sent for the man's parents. [19] "Is this your son?" they asked. "Is this the one you say was born blind? How is it that now he can see?"

[20] "We know he is our son," the parents answered, "and we know he was born blind. [21] But how he can see now, or who opened his eyes, we don't know. Ask him. He is of age; he will speak for himself." [22] His parents said this because they were afraid of the Jews, for already the Jews had decided that anyone who acknowledged that Jesus was the Christ would be put out of the synagogue. [23] That was why his parents said, "He is of age; ask him."

[24] A second time they summoned the man who had been blind. "Give glory to God," they said. "We know this man is a sinner."

Good answer! When you get put on the spot about Jesus, don't get bogged down in theology. **Just tell what he has done for you!**

[25] He replied, "Whether he is a sinner or not, I don't know. One thing I do know. I was blind but now I see!"

[26] Then they asked him, "What did he do to you? How did he open your eyes?"

[27] He answered, "I have told you already and you

did not listen. Why do you want to hear it again? Do you want to become his disciples, too?"

28 Then they hurled insults at him and said, "You are this fellow's disciple! We are disciples of Moses! 29 We know that God spoke to Moses, but as for this fellow, we don't even know where he comes from."

30 The man answered, "Now that is remarkable! You don't know where he comes from, yet he opened my eyes. 31 We know that God does not listen to sinners. He listens to the godly man who does his will. 32 Nobody has ever heard of opening the eyes of a man born blind. 33 If this man were not from God, he could do nothing."

34 To this they replied, "You were steeped in sin at birth; how dare you lecture us!" And they threw him out.

35 Jesus heard that they had thrown him out, and when he found him, he said, ("Do you believe in the Son of Man?")

36 "Who is he, sir?" the man asked. "Tell me so that I may believe in him."

37 Jesus said, "You have now seen him; in fact, he is the one speaking with you."

38 Then the man said, "Lord, I believe," and he worshipped him.

39 Jesus said, "For judgment I have come into this world, so that the blind will see and those who see will become blind."

40 Some Pharisees who were with him heard him say this and asked, "What? Are we blind too?"

41 Jesus said, "If you were blind, you would not be guilty of sin; but now that you claim you can see, your guilt remains.)

Nice one!

This statement makes my blood boil! They asked him what happened, he told them the truth, they didn't like it! To show it they heaped a load of abuse on him. But one thing thay cannot change -he can see! YES!!!

Who do you say Jesus is?

The Pharisees claimed to know God but were spiritually blind.

the good shepherd

"I tell you the truth, the man who does not enter the sheep pen by the gate, but climbs in by some other way, is a thief and a robber. [2] The man who enters by the gate is the shepherd of his sheep. [3] The watchman opens the gate for him, and the sheep listen to his voice. He calls his own sheep by name and leads them out. [4] When he has brought out all his own, he goes on ahead of them, and his sheep follow him because they know his voice. [5] But they will never follow a stranger; in fact, they will run away from him because they do not recognise a stranger's voice." [6] Jesus used this figure of speech, but they did not understand what he was telling them.

[7] Therefore Jesus said again, "I tell you the truth, I am the gate for the sheep. [8] All who ever came before me were thieves and robbers, but the sheep did not listen to them. [9] I am the gate; whoever enters through me will be saved. He will come in and go out, and find pasture. [10] The thief comes only to steal and kill and destroy; I have come that they may have life, and have it to the full.

[11] "I am the good shepherd. The good shepherd lays down his life for the sheep. [12] The hired hand is not the shepherd who owns the sheep. So when he sees the wolf coming, he abandons the sheep and runs away. Then the

SHEPHERD

In Palestine, the shepherd walked in front of his sheep, leading them into fresh pasture. They recognised his voice, responding only to him. The sheep pen was surrounded by walls, but open to the sky. The shepherd lay in the one opening at night, physically laying his life between them and any danger through the night.

See verse 17.

wolf attacks the flock and scatters it. [13] The man runs away because he is a `hired hand` and cares nothing for the sheep.

[14] "I am the good shepherd; I know my sheep and my sheep know me— [15] just as the Father knows me and I know the Father—and I lay down my life for the sheep. [16] I have other sheep that are not of this sheep pen. I must bring them also. They too will listen to my voice, and there shall be one flock and one shepherd. [17] The reason my Father loves me is that I lay down my life—only to take it up again. [18] No-one takes it from me, but I lay it down of my own accord. I have authority to lay it down and authority to take it up again. This command I received from my Father."

[19] At these words the Jews were again divided. [20] Many of them said, "He is demon-possessed and raving mad. Why listen to him?"

[21] But others said, "These are not the sayings of a man possessed by a demon. Can a demon open the eyes of the blind?"

[22] Then came the Feast of Dedication at Jerusalem. It was winter, [23] and Jesus was in the temple area walking in Solomon's Colonnade. [24] The Jews gathered round him, saying, "How long will you keep us in suspense? If you are the Christ, tell us plainly."

[25] Jesus answered, "I did tell you, but you do not believe. The miracles I do in my Father's name speak for me, [26] but you do not believe because you are not my sheep. [27] My sheep listen to my voice; I know them, and they follow me. [28] I give them eternal life, and they shall never perish; no-one can snatch them out of my hand. [29] My Father, who has given them to me, is greater than all; no-one can snatch them out

Reference to the resurrection. JB

Good Point!!

See page 44

Jesus is the only **ETERNAL** life insurance!!

Jesus making a direct claim to be God!!

"That's the point guys...
I am God!"

Hmmm.... This is Jesus beating the boffs at their own game. There's a bit in Psalm 82 v6 where the judges are referred to as "gods". I've a sneaky feeling Jesus is employing a bit of sarcasm here - the judges obviously behaved like little tin-pot dictators and were totally unfair.

Jesus is asking "are you going to accuse the guy who wrote the psalm of blasphemy as well? At least I really am God!"

Jesus was who he says he was.

of my Father's hand. [30] "I and the Father are one."

[31] Again the Jews picked up stones to stone him, [32] but Jesus said to them, "I have shown you many great miracles from the Father. For which of these do you stone me?"

[33] "We are not stoning you for any of these," replied the Jews, "but for blasphemy, because you, a mere man, claim to be God."

[34] Jesus answered them, "Is it not written in your Law, 'I have said you are gods'? [35] If he called them 'gods', to whom the word of God came—and the Scripture cannot be broken—[36] what about the one whom the Father set apart as his very own and sent into the world? Why then do you accuse me of blasphemy because I said, 'I am God's Son'? [37] Do not believe me unless I do what my Father does. [38] But if I do it, even though you do not believe me, believe the miracles, that you may know and understand that the Father is in me, and I in the Father." [39] Again they tried to seize him, but he escaped their grasp.

[40] Then Jesus went back across the Jordan to the place where John had been baptising in the early days. Here he stayed [41] and many people came to him. They said, "Though John never performed a miraculous sign, all that John said about this man was true." [42] And in that place many believed in Jesus.

Happy Fibre?

Feast of Dedication: Called **Hanukkah,** the feast of dedication is still celebrated by Jews today. It commemorates the time (164 B.C.) when a heroic bloke called Judas the Maccabee recaptured the temple from a nasty piece of work called Antiochus Epiphanes who thought it was funny to burn pigs on God's altar. **(God didn't think so.)** This dedication was a purification ceremony for the desecrated temple.

chapter 11
LAZARUS
the facts

Now a man named Lazarus was sick. He was from Bethany, the village of Mary and her sister Martha. ² This Mary, whose brother Lazarus now lay sick, was the same one who poured perfume on the Lord and wiped his feet with her hair. ³ So the sisters sent word to Jesus, "Lord, the one you love is sick."

⁴ When he heard this, Jesus said, "This sickness will not end in death. No, it is for God's glory so that God's Son may be glorified through it." ⁵ Jesus loved Martha and her sister and Lazarus. ⁶ Yet when he heard that Lazarus was sick, he stayed where he was two more days.

⁷ Then he said to his disciples, "Let us go back to Judea."

⁸ "But Rabbi," they said, "a short while ago the Jews tried to stone you, and yet you are going back there?"

⁹ Jesus answered, "Are there not twelve hours of daylight? A man who walks by day will not stumble, for he sees by this world's light. ¹⁰ It is when he walks by night that he stumbles, for he has no light."

¹¹ After he had said this, he went on to tell them, "Our friend Lazarus has fallen asleep; but I am going there to wake him up."

¹² His disciples replied, "Lord, if he sleeps, he will get better." ¹³ Jesus had been speaking of his death, but his disciples thought he meant natural sleep.

¹⁴ So then he told them plainly, "Lazarus is dead,

See the rest of the story in John Ch12.

Jesus knew exactly what he was doing because of his close relationship with the Father. *We do not stumble when we are close to the Father and are listening to God's voice.*

Thomas and Didymus both mean twin.

Thomas was not known for his optimism, but Jesus' life was now seriously at risk from the powerful religious leaders.

Martha knew that Jesus could have healed her brother whilst he was still alive.

When I believe in Jesus, even though my physical body will die, I will live for ever!!!! Amazing!!

Martha had no doubt who Jesus was, even though he didn't seem to have come up with the goods.

¹⁵and for your sake I am glad I was not there, so that you may believe. But let us go to him."

¹⁶Then Thomas (called Didymus) said to the rest of the disciples, "Let us also go, that we may die with him."

¹⁷On his arrival, Jesus found that Lazarus had already been in the tomb for four days. ¹⁸Bethany was less than two miles from Jerusalem, ¹⁹and many Jews had come to Martha and Mary to comfort them in the loss of their brother. ²⁰When Martha heard that Jesus was coming, she went out to meet him, but Mary stayed at home.

²¹"Lord," Martha said to Jesus, "if you had been here, my brother would not have died." ²²But I know that even now God will give you whatever you ask."

²³Jesus said to her, "Your brother will rise again."

²⁴Martha answered, "I know he will rise again in the resurrection at the last day."

²⁵Jesus said to her, "I am the resurrection and the life. He who believes in me will live, even though he dies; ²⁶and whoever lives and believes in me will never die. Do you believe this?"

²⁷"Yes, Lord," she told him, "I believe that you are the Christ, the Son of God, who was to come into the world."

²⁸And after she had said this, she went back and called her sister Mary aside. "The Teacher is here,"

High Fibre?

Burial Jewish Style: At the time of Jesus, the custom was to embalm the dead body in strips of cloth, using various spices and ointments. The body was then laid on a stone shelf in the tomb.

The tomb was often a man-made cave with a stone which was rolled across the entrance. After a year or so, the remains (mostly bones) were put into a stone box to make room for the next member of the family.

she said, "and is asking for you." [29] When Mary heard this, she got up quickly and went to him. [30] Now Jesus had not yet entered the village, but was still at the place where Martha had met him. [31] When the Jews who had been with Mary in the house, comforting her, noticed how quickly she got up and went out, they followed her, supposing she was going to the tomb to mourn there.

[32] When Mary reached the place where Jesus was and saw him, she fell at his feet and said, "Lord, if you had been here, my brother would not have died."

[33] When Jesus saw her weeping, and the Jews who had come along with her also weeping, he was deeply moved in spirit and troubled. [34] "Where have you laid him?" he asked.

"Come and see, Lord," they replied.

[35] Jesus wept.

[36] Then the Jews said, "See how he loved him!"

[37] But some of them said, "Could not he who opened the eyes of the blind man have kept this man from dying?"

[38] Jesus, once more deeply moved, came to the tomb. It was a cave with a stone laid across the entrance. [39] "Take away the stone," he said.

"But, Lord," said Martha, the sister of the dead man, "by this time there is a bad odour, for he has been there four days."

[40] Then Jesus said, "Did I not tell you that if you believed, you would see the glory of God?"

[41] So they took away the stone. Then Jesus looked up and said, "Father, I thank you that you have heard me. [42] I knew that you always hear me, but I said this for the benefit of the people standing here, that they may believe that you sent me."

Jesus was very close to the family and Mary's grief moved him. But, it was more than just feeling sorry for her, "he was deeply moved in spirit".

Was this a signal to Jesus from the Holy Spirit to get into action?

The shortest verse in the Bible. God has emotions: he made us like himself.

The glory of God broke out that day in a way that family would never forget!

Chapter · 12 · · 48·49

Only the one who gave life in the first place could bring someone back after being dead for four days! Read Ch 1 v3
You would think that eveyone would have accepted him by now!

You won't believe what he's gone and done? He's only raised the dead!

The chief priests and the Pharisees were worried about losing their power and influence if everyone turned to Jesus.

The Lamb of God who takes away the sin of the world. See Ch 1 v29.

⁴³ When he had said this, Jesus called in a loud voice, "Lazarus, come out!" ⁴⁴ The dead man came out, his hands and feet wrapped with strips of linen, and a cloth around his face.

Jesus said to them, "Take off the grave clothes and let him go."

⁴⁵ Therefore many of the Jews who had come to visit Mary, and had seen what Jesus did, put their faith in him. ⁴⁶ But some of them went to the Pharisees and told them what Jesus had done. ⁴⁷ Then the chief priests and the Pharisees called a meeting of the Sanhedrin.

"What are we accomplishing?" they asked. "Here is this man performing many miraculous signs. ⁴⁸ If we let him go on like this, everyone will believe in him, and then the Romans will come and take away both our place and our nation."

⁴⁹ Then one of them, named Caiaphas, who was high priest that year, spoke up, "You know nothing at all! ⁵⁰ You do not realise that it is better for you that one man die for the people than that the whole nation perish."

⁵¹ He did not say this on his own, but as high priest that year he prophesied that Jesus would die for the Jewish nation, ⁵² and not only for that nation but also for the scattered children of God, to bring them together and make them one. ⁵³ So from that day on they plotted to take his life.

⁵⁴ Therefore Jesus no longer moved about publicly among the Jews. Instead he withdrew to a region near the desert, to a village called Ephraim, where he stayed with his disciples.

⁵⁵ When it was almost time for the Jewish Passover, many went up from the country to

Jerusalem for their ceremonial cleansing before the Passover. [56] They kept looking for Jesus, and as they stood in the temple area they asked one another, "What do you think? Isn't he coming to the Feast at all?" [57] But the chief priests and Pharisees had given orders that if anyone found out where Jesus was, he should report it so that they might arrest him.

CHAPTER 12

Smells with attitude.

Passover - see Ch 6 and notes on page 29.

Six days before the Passover, Jesus arrived at Bethany, where Lazarus lived, whom Jesus had raised from the dead. [2] Here a dinner was given in Jesus' honour. Martha served, while Lazarus was among those reclining at the table with him. [3] Then Mary took about a pint of pure nard, an expensive perfume; she poured it on Jesus' feet and wiped his feet with her hair. And the house was filled with the fragrance of the perfume.

[4] But one of his disciples, Judas Iscariot, who was later to betray him, objected, [5] "Why wasn't this perfume sold and the money given to the poor? It was worth a year's wages." [6] He did not say this because he cared about the poor but because he was a thief; as keeper of the money bag, he used to help himself to what was put into it.

High Fibre?

Smelly Worship!!! - Mary got a bit carried away as she splashed the Chanel no.5 all over Jesus' feet! The amazing thing was that Jesus was not embarrassed at all! - I bet some of the disciples were! Jesus accepted it as true worship.

To worship is to express our love and devotion to God. The Bible makes the comparison between God's love for us and our love for him with that of two lovers. (Read Song of Songs in the O.T.) **Worship is from the heart and can be totally spontaneous.**

Just as the perfume had a lovely smell, so our worship is a beautiful fragrance to God.

(see Revelation Ch 5 v8, Ch 8 w3,4)

Jesus never had a proper burial, he was placed in a borrowed tomb at the last minute - everyone wanted to knock off work ready for the special Sabbath which followed the Passover.

"Let's try and destroy the evidence!"- Doing the work of their father the devil. Since day one he's been trying to destroy Jesus. Read also Matthew Ch 4 vv1-11

Riding a donkey is not exactly a macho way for a king to enter the capital city! A chauffeur-driven camel and body guards wearing sunglasses and tea towels on their heads would have been a bit more spectacular!!

Jesus was making a point as well as fulfilling a bit of prophecy. He is not like any other king. He doesn't need glamour and macho-stuff to be the greatest in the universe!

⁷ "Leave her alone," Jesus replied. "It was intended, that she should save this perfume for the day of my burial. ⁸ You will always have the poor among you, but you will not always have me."

⁹ Meanwhile a large crowd of Jews found out that Jesus was there and came, not only because of him but also to see Lazarus, whom he had raised from the dead. ¹⁰ So the chief priests made plans to kill Lazarus as well, ¹¹ for on account of him many of the Jews were going over to Jesus and putting their faith in him.

¹² The next day the great crowd that had come for the Feast heard that Jesus was on his way to Jerusalem. ¹³ They took palm branches and went out to meet him, shouting,

"Hosanna!"

"Blessed is he who comes in the name of
the Lord!"

"Blessed is the King of Israel!"

¹⁴ Jesus found a young donkey and sat upon it, as it is written,

¹⁵ "Do not be afraid, O Daughter
of Zion;
see, your king is coming,
seated on a donkey's colt."

¹⁶ At first his disciples did not understand all this. Only after Jesus was glorified did they realise that these things had been written about him and that they had done these things to him.

¹⁷ Now the crowd that was with him when he called Lazarus from the tomb and raised him from the dead continued to spread the word. ¹⁸ Many

people, because they had heard that he had given this miraculous sign, went out to meet him. ¹⁹ So the Pharisees said to one another, "See, this is getting us nowhere. Look how the whole world has gone after him!"

²⁰ Now there were some Greeks among those who went up to worship at the Feast. ²¹ They came to Philip, who was from Bethsaida in Galilee, with a request. "Sir," they said, "we would like to see Jesus." ²² Philip went to tell Andrew; Andrew and Philip in turn told Jesus.

²³ Jesus replied, "The hour has come for the Son of Man to be glorified." ²⁴ I tell you the truth, unless a grain of wheat falls to the ground and dies, it remains only a single seed. But if it dies, it produces many seeds. ²⁵ The man who loves his life will lose it, while the man who hates his life in this world will keep it for eternal life. ²⁶ Whoever serves me must follow me; and where I am, my servant also will be. My Father will honour the one who serves me.

²⁷ "Now my heart is troubled, and what shall I say? 'Father, save me from this hour'? No, it was for this very reason I came to this hour. ²⁸ Father, glorify your name!"

Then a voice came from heaven, "I have glorified it, and will glorify it again."

The Greeks were non-Jews, Gentiles. Until this time Jesus had only reached the Jews and Samaritans. Suddenly the Gentile world was coming to him. (See also v19). *Isaiah prophesied 700 years before this that Jesus would be a "light for the Gentiles".*

It seems that the Greeks' coming was a sign to Jesus that things were reaching a climax and that his crucifixion was near.

High Fibre?

Seeds - There is an important principle seen in planting seeds. Until you plant say, a piece of corn, it is only one piece of corn. Yeah, Pretty obvious so far! Well, if you were to hang onto that piece of corn and not bury it in the soil, you will only ever have one measly bit of corn!

If you do plant it, it will "die", but out of it will come an ear of corn. That is the principle Jesus operated when he died. If he had clung to his own life nobody would have had the long-term benefit from his life on earth.

When we are born again we are saying "I want to let go of my own life and lose it to find the eternal life Jesus has for me".

The reality of what is ahead is starting to sink in. Jesus was fully human (although fully God too), so the future must have felt pretty scary!

"The prince of this world" refers to the devil or satan. He has had power over the human race ever since Adam and Eve followed his snakey suggestions in the Garden of Eden!
(See Genesis Ch 3 & Romans Ch 5 v12).

Jesus' death was to break Satan's stranglehold on the world totally.

While Jesus was physically present on the earth, **it was like the light was on.** It is a lot easier to make sense of things with the light on than in the dark!

Wow!!! - How much more could he do? But they had chosen not to believe!

²⁹ The crowd that was there and heard it said it had thundered; others said an angel had spoken to him.

³⁰ Jesus said, "This voice was for your benefit, not mine. ³¹ Now is the time for judgment on this world; now the prince of this world will be driven out. ³² But I, when I am lifted up from the earth, will draw all men to myself." ³³ He said this to show the kind of death he was going to die.

³⁴ The crowd spoke up, "We have heard from the Law that the Christ will remain for ever, so how can you say, 'The Son of Man must be lifted up'? Who is this 'Son of Man'?"

³⁵ Then Jesus told them, "You are going to have the light just a little while longer. Walk while you have the light, before darkness overtakes you. The man who walks in the dark does not know where he is going. ³⁶ Put your trust in the light while you have it, so that you may become sons of light." When he had finished speaking, Jesus left and hid himself from them.

³⁷ Even after Jesus had done all these miraculous signs in their presence, they still would not believe in him. ³⁸ This was to fulfil the word of Isaiah the prophet:

"Lord, who has believed our message
    and to whom has the arm of the Lord
        been revealed?"

³⁹ For this reason they could not believe, because, as Isaiah says elsewhere:

⁴⁰ "He has blinded their eyes
    and deadened their hearts,
so they can neither with their eyes,
    nor understand with their hearts,

nor turn—and I would heal them."

[41] Isaiah said this because he saw Jesus' glory and spoke about him.

[42] Yet at the same time many even among the leaders believed in him. But because of the Pharisees they would not confess their faith for fear they would be put out of the synagogue; [43] for they loved praise from men more than praise from God.

[44] Then Jesus cried out, "When a man believes in me, he does not believe in me only, but in the one who sent me. [45] When he looks at me, he sees the one who sent me. [46] I have come into the world as a light, so that no-one who believes in me should stay in darkness.

[47] "As for the person who hears my words but does not keep them, I do not judge him. For I did not come to judge the world, but to save it. [48] There is a judge for the one who rejects me and does not accept my words; that very word which I spoke will condemn him at the last day. [49] For I did not speak of my own accord, but the Father who sent me commanded me what to say and how to say it. [50] I know that his command leads to eternal life. So whatever I say is just what the Father has told me to say."

700 years before!!

Many of us care more about what people think of us than about what God thinks.
BIG mistake!!

Peer group pressure will often keep people away from Jesus and all the good stuff he wants to do with them!

Jesus took a lot on the chin for me. Ask yourself: Am I ready...?

"The Word"
remember Ch 1?

Jesus washes their... **feet.**

Chapter 13

It was just before the Passover Feast. Jesus knew that the time had come for him to leave this world and go to the Father. Having loved his own who were in the world, he now showed them the full extent of his love.

² The evening meal was being served, and the devil had already prompted Judas Iscariot, son of Simon, to betray Jesus. ³ Jesus knew that the Father had put all things under his power, and that he had come

Wet Fibre?

Foot washing: -Jesus was totally secure in himself: he knew who he was, where he had come from and where he was going. He had no fear of losing face in front of his disciples!

Jesus was doing the job of a servant in washing the grime off his disciples' cheesy feet! What he was also doing was saying "this is what my whole life has been about. I came not to be served but to serve. God himself has been among you as a servant, to demonstrate the mind-blowing love that God has for the people he made! This is what my kingdom is about and this is how I want you to treat each other."

from God and was returning to God; [4] so he got up from the meal, took off his outer clothing, and wrapped a towel round his waist. [5] After that, he poured water into a basin and began to wash his disciples' feet, drying them with the towel that was wrapped round him.

[6] He came to Simon Peter, who said to him, "Lord, are you going to wash my feet?"

[7] Jesus replied, "You do not realise now what I am doing, but later you will understand."

[8] "No," said Peter, "you shall never wash my feet."

Jesus answered, "Unless I wash you, you have no part with me."

[9] "Then, Lord," Simon Peter replied, "not just my feet but my hands and my head as well!"

[10] Jesus answered, "A person who has had a bath needs only to wash his feet; his whole body is clean. And you are clean, though not every one of you." [11] For he knew who was going to betray him, and that was why he said not every one was clean.

[12] When he had finished washing their feet, he put on his clothes and returned to his place. "Do you understand what I have done for you?" he asked them. [13] "You call me 'Teacher' and 'Lord', and rightly so, for that is what I am. [14] Now that I, your Lord and Teacher, have washed your feet, you also should wash one another's feet. [15] I have set you an example that you should do as I have done for you. [16] I tell you the truth, no servant is greater than his master, nor is a messenger greater than the one who sent him. [17] Now that you know these things, you will be blessed if you do them.

[18] "I am not referring to all of you; I know those I have chosen. But this is to fulfil the scripture: 'He

The feet get messy pretty quickly, especially if you wear sandals. Jesus makes our whole "inner self" clean when we are born again, but we still get grubby from our day to day contact with the world.

We need to come to Jesus daily for a wash!

The messenger represents the one who sent him. As we serve each other and the people we meet, we are demonstrating Jesus' love to the world.

Jesus again lets on that he knows all about Judas. In sharing bread with him he was saying "I entrust myself to you".

The disciple Jesus loved was John - *yeah, the guy who wrote this book!*

If there was one person in history you would swap places with, would it be John?

The act of betraying Jesus was such an evil thing to do, the devil himself got directly involved in Judas' life at this point. Judas literally sold his soul to the devil!

John includes those minute details which stick in the mind when we witness events.

who shares my bread has lifted up his heel against me.'

¹⁹ "I am telling you now before it happens, so that when it does happen you will believe that I am He. ²⁰ I tell you the truth, whoever accepts anyone I send accepts me; and whoever accepts me accepts the one who sent me."

²¹ After he had said this, Jesus was troubled in spirit and testified, "I tell you the truth, one of you is going to betray me."

²² His disciples stared at one another, at a loss to know which of them he meant. ²³ One of them, the disciple whom Jesus loved, was reclining next to him. ²⁴ Simon Peter motioned to this disciple and said, "Ask him which one he means."

²⁵ Leaning back against Jesus, he asked him, "Lord, who is it?"

²⁶ Jesus answered, "It is the one to whom I will give this piece of bread when I have dipped it in the dish." Then, dipping the piece of bread, he gave it to Judas Iscariot, son of Simon. ²⁷ As soon as Judas took the bread, Satan entered into him.

"What you are about to do, do quickly," Jesus told him, ²⁸ but no-one at the meal understood why Jesus said this to him. ²⁹ Since Judas had charge of the money, some thought Jesus was telling him to buy what was needed for the Feast, or to give something to the poor. ³⁰ As soon as Judas had taken the bread, he went out. And it was night.

³¹ When he was gone, Jesus said, "Now is the Son of Man glorified and God is glorified in him. ³² If God is glorified in him, God will glorify the Son in himself, and will glorify him at once.

³³ "My children, I will be with you only a little longer. You will look for me, and just as I told the Jews, so I tell you now: Where I am going, you cannot come.

³⁴ "A new command I give you: (Love one another.) As I have loved you, so you must love one another. ³⁵By this all men will know that you are my disciples, if you love one another."

³⁶ Simon Peter asked him, "Lord, where are you going?"

Jesus replied, "Where I am going, you cannot follow now, but you will follow later."

³⁷ Peter asked, "Lord, why can't I follow you now? I will lay down my life for you."

³⁸ Then Jesus answered, "Will you really lay down your life for me? I tell you the truth, before the cock crows, you will disown me three times!

As Jesus willingly accepted the pain of Judas' betrayal he showed more of God's glory in himself - that God would suffer such rejection to save mankind.

Selfless love is the thing which marks out true disciples of Jesus

Even brave old Peter would deny he knew Jesus.

Chapter 14
Jesus encourages the team

"Do not let your hearts be troubled. Trust in God; trust also in me. ² In my Father's house are many rooms; if it were not so, I would have told you. I am going there to prepare a place for you. ³ And if I go and prepare a place for you, I will come back and take you to be with me that you also may be where I am. ⁴ You know the way to the place where I am going."

⁵ Thomas said to him, "Lord, we don't know where you are going, so how can we know the way?"

The disciples were getting a little anxious, not fully understanding everything Jesus was saying and hinting at, so Jesus gives them a glimpse of the end of the story. The end purpose of it all was that his disciples (including present day ones) would spend for ever, eternity with Jesus in the Father's house.

New-Age thinking says "Find your own way, every path leads to God so if it feels good for you that's O.K.!" **Well sorry, Jesus said it's not O.K.!** He said no-one comes to the Father except through him.

Not a very 90's thing to say really! But, somethings never change however unpopular they seem!

Jesus is God expressed in a language everyone can understand. - not a load of theological stuff you need a degree to unravel!!

We can do the stuff Jesus spent his time doing: healing, miracles etc. if we have faith in him. That means knowing that it's his power not our own and that he will deliver the goods! **If we stay close to God, listening to him and doing what he says our lives can be like Jesus' life.**

⁶ Jesus answered, "I am the way and the truth and the life. No-one comes to the Father except through me. ⁷ If you really knew me, you would know my Father as well. From now on, you do know him and have seen him."

⁸ Philip said, "Lord, show us the Father and that will be enough for us."

⁹ Jesus answered: "Don't you know me, Philip, even after I have been among you such a long time? Anyone who has seen me has seen the Father. How can you say, 'Show us the Father'? ¹⁰ Don't you believe that I am in the Father, and that the Father is in me? The words I say to you are not just my own. Rather, it is the Father, living in me, who is doing his work. ¹¹ Believe me when I say that I am in the Father and the Father is in me; or at least believe on the evidence of the miracles themselves. ¹² I tell you the truth, anyone who has faith in me will do what I have been doing. He will do even greater things than these, because I am going to the Father. ¹³ And I will do whatever you ask in my name, so that the Son may bring glory to the Father. ¹⁴ You may ask me for anything in my name, and I will do it.

"In Jesus' name" is not like saying "lots of love" at the end of a letter. Jesus is saying when we ask God for things we have access to him through Jesus. It's like Jesus has given us his PIN number to his Father's bank account! Jesus says "ask me"- he provides a direct line to the **Boss**. Pretty impressive eh??

¹⁵ "If you love me, you will obey what I command. ¹⁶ And I will ask the Father, and he will give you another Counsellor to be with you for ever— ¹⁷ the Spirit of truth. The world cannot accept him, because it neither sees him nor knows him. But you know him, for he lives with you and will be in you. ¹⁸ I will not leave you as orphans; I will come to you. ¹⁹ Before long, the world will not see me any more, but you will see me. Because I live, you also will live. ²⁰ On that day you will realise that I am in my Father, and you are in me, and I am in you. ²¹ Whoever has my commands and obeys them, he is the one who loves me. He who loves me will be loved by my Father, and I too will love him and show myself to him."

²² Then Judas (not Judas Iscariot) said, "But, Lord, why do you intend to show yourself to us and not to the world?"

²³ Jesus replied, "If anyone loves me, he will obey my teaching. My Father will love him, and we will come to him and make our home with him. ²⁴ He who does not love me will not obey my teaching. These words you hear are not my own; they belong to the Father who sent me.

²⁵ "All this I have spoken while still with you. ²⁶ But the Counsellor, the Holy Spirit, whom the Father will send in my name, will teach you all things and will remind you of everything I have said to you. ²⁷ Peace I leave with you; my peace I give you. I do not give to you as the world gives. Do not let your hearts be troubled and do not be afraid.

High Fibre?

The Holy Spirit, (JB) Ch 3 v8, is like the wind. But he is much more (the wind is just a force): **the Holy Spirit is God!!!** "Counsellor" is another name for the Holy Spirit. **The Greek word means "another helper the same as me".** The Holy Spirit teaches us internally. He makes the words of Jesus and the Bible come alive. Without him the Bible is just a pile of dusty writings from a bunch of dead people! **If it doesn't make sense ask the Holy Spirit.**

v23 God has always wanted to live closely with his people. See the ultimate result - Revelation Ch 21 v3: **"Now the dwelling of God is with men, and he will live with them. They will be his people, and God himself will be with them and be their God."**

Peace man!!

Forget flower power - **Jesus is the Prince of Peace!** - Peace with God, sin washed away, freedom to be the person God made me. **What human peace comes near that?**

The devil was about to have his biggest moment in history - the death of Jesus. But, Jesus knew that the devil had no real power over him. *Jesus had never given way, even one teeny bit!*

28 "You heard me say, 'I am going away and I am coming back to you.' If you loved me, you would be glad that I am going to the Father, for the Father is greater than I. 29 I have told you now before it happens, so that when it does happen you will believe. 30 I will not speak with you much longer, for the prince of this world is coming. He has no hold on me, 31 but the world must learn that I love the Father and that I do exactly what my Father has commanded me.

"Come now; let us leave.

Gardener's World: The Bible uses all sorts of pictures and comparisons as means of illustrating the point. Jesus is saying in Chapter 15 that he is like a grapevine and his followers are like branches growing out from him.

It's a good picture, because a vine branch cannot grow grapes unless it's joined to the stump. The stump is what has the roots and what supplies life to the rest of the plant. If we are to live **fruitful lives** we must be well-hooked into Jesus - he's the one who supplies the life.

"Remaining in him" means, not getting dragged away by the pull of the world outside; by worry, fear, dodgy relationships, ambition etc; but by staying close to Jesus. In any relationship it's good to talk. **Talk to Jesus!** Share the good stuff and the bad stuff with him. Remember, he has the power to change things! **Expect him to speak back** - through the Bible, but also by the quiet inner voice of the **Holy Spirit**.

Fruity Bit: What is fruit? It is the reason an apple tree or a grapevine is planted.

They may look pretty nice as well, but that's a bonus. The fruit of Jesus' life was that people discovered that God loved them. As they came into contact with Jesus they were overwhelmed by his kindness and love. **As we hang around with Jesus the same thing will happen through our lives!**

The Holy Spirit inside us brings the goodness of Jesus out in our lives - known as "The Fruit of the Spirit", **(See Galatians Ch 5 v22)**

Pruning: I bet the grapevine doesn't go a bunch on pruning - sounds a bit painful!! Sometimes God gets his pruning knife out with us! If there is stuff in our lives which is making us less fruitful - bad habits, destructive friendships etc - God will prod us until we get them sorted!

Clear-up Time v 6 People who insist on staying away from Jesus, will not only be unfruitful, but they will also lose everything ultimately. The day will come when Jesus clears up the garden and has to dispose of all those who have wilfully rejected him.

"I am the true vine, and my Father is the gardener. [2] He cuts off every branch in me that bears no fruit, while every branch that does bear fruit he prunes so that it will be even more fruitful. [3] You are already clean because of the word I have spoken to you. [4] Remain in me, and I will remain in you. No branch can bear fruit by itself; it must remain in the vine. Neither can you bear fruit unless you remain in me.

[5] "I am the vine; you are the branches. If a man remains in me and I in him, he will bear much fruit; apart from me you can do nothing. [6] If anyone does not remain in me, he is like a branch that is thrown away and withers; such branches are picked up, thrown into the fire and burned. [7] If you remain in me and my words remain in you, ask whatever you wish, and it will be given you. [8] This is to my Father's glory, that you bear much fruit, showing yourselves to be my disciples.

[9] "As the Father has loved me, so have I loved you. Now remain in my love. [10] If you obey my commands, you will remain in my love, just as I have obeyed my Father's commands and remain in his love. [11] I have told you this so that my joy may be in you and that your joy may be complete. [12] My command is this: Love each other as I have loved you. [13] Greater love has no-one than this, that he lay down his life for his friends. [14] You are my friends if you do what I command. [15] I no longer call you servants, because a servant does not know his master's business. Instead, I have called you friends, for everything that I learned from my Father I have made known to you. [16] You did not choose me, but I chose you and appointed you to go and bear fruit—fruit that will last. Then the Father will give you whatever you ask in my name. [17] This is my command: Love each other.

If we stay *close* to Jesus and keep in mind his words, we will pray the kind of prayers he would pray – God always answered Jesus' prayers!

Jesus will never stop loving us, but drifting into sin will stop us enjoying his love. When a child is naughty, parents may show love by some kind of discipline!
Jesus never drifted away from his Father's love.

Jesus died for us when we couldn't have cared less about him!

Jesus wants us to be his friends.

WILD

Hated by the World?
If Jesus made people feel uncomfortable, we may cause the same reaction!

Warning! Try not to get jip for just being a plain old pain in the neck – there's no benefit to anyone in that!

When Jesus speaks to us we no longer have an excuse for ignoring him, and staying put in our sin.

The Holy Spirit will always draw attention to Jesus. He will also seriously help us when we speak about Jesus. (See Mark Ch 13 v11).

Chapter

A bit drastic!... Some countries will kill you if you openly worship Jesus. In the U.K. people from certain ethnic backgrounds who turn to Jesus can face total isolation from their family.

18 "If the world hates you, keep in mind that it hated me first. 19 If you belonged to the world, it would love you as its own. As it is, you do not belong to the world, but I have chosen you out of the world. That is why the world hates you. 20 Remember the words I spoke to you: 'No servant is greater than his master.' If they persecuted me, they will persecute you also. If they obeyed my teaching, they will obey yours also. 21 They will treat you this way because of my name, for they do not know the One who sent me. 22 If I had not come and spoken to them, they would not be guilty of sin. Now, however, they have no excuse for their sin. 23 He who hates me hates my Father as well. 24 If I had not done among them what no-one else did, they would not be guilty of sin. But now they have seen these miracles, and yet they have hated both me and my Father. 25 But this is to fulfil what is written in their Law: 'They hated me without reason.'

26 "When the Counsellor comes, whom I will send to you from the Father, the Spirit of truth who goes out from the Father, he will testify about me. 27 And you also must testify, for you have been with me from the beginning.

16 "All this I have told you so that you will not go astray. 2 They will put you out of the synagogue; in fact, a time is coming when anyone who kills you will think he is offering a service to God. 3 They will do such things because they have not known the Father or me. 4 I have told you this, so that when the time comes you will remember that I warned you. I did not tell you this at first because I was with you.

⁵ "Now I am going to him who sent me, yet none of you asks me, 'Where are you going?' ⁶ Because I have said these things, you are filled with grief. ⁷ But I tell you the truth: It is for your good that I am going away. Unless I go away, the Counsellor will not come to you; but if I go, I will send him to you. ⁸ When he comes, he will convict the world of guilt in regard to sin and righteousness and judgment: ⁹ in regard to sin, because men do not believe in me; ¹⁰ in regard to righteousness, because I am going to the Father, where you can see me no longer; ¹¹ and in regard to judgment, because the prince of this world now stands condemned.

¹² "I have much more to say to you, more than you can now bear. ¹³ But when he, the Spirit of truth, comes, he will guide you into all truth. He will not speak on his own; he will speak only what he hears, and he will tell you what is yet to come. ¹⁴ He will bring glory to me by taking from what is mine and making it known to you. ¹⁵ All that belongs to the Father is mine. That is why I said the Spirit will take from what is mine and make it known to you.

¹⁶ "In a little while you will see me no more, and then after a little while you will see me."

¹⁷ Some of his disciples said to one another, "What does he mean by saying, 'In a little while you will see me no more, and then after a little while you will see me,' and 'Because I am going to the Father'?" ¹⁸ They kept asking, "What does he mean by 'a little while'? We don't understand what he is saying."

¹⁹ Jesus saw that they wanted to ask him about this, so he said to them, "Are you asking

It may not be a popular decision if you choose to follow Jesus!

Jesus could not send the Holy Spirit until he had returned to the Father – "mission accomplished!"

High Fibre?

More on the Holy Spirit: Part of the job of the Holy Spirit is to make people aware of their sinful state and of their need for Jesus. We can pray for people that God will work on them by his Spirit.

It is his job to carry on teaching and speaking to us as Jesus would if he was here. All the things we need to know and understand about God he will teach us. He will teach us as we read the words of Jesus in this Gospel and in the Bible. He will guide us inwardly as we make decisions, he will make us feel uncomfortable about sin and he will bring us into the lifestyle God wants us to live.

Like any good friend we can shut him up by totally ignoring him! **Big mistake!** A really smart person will let the Holy Spirit be the guv'nor!

If you haven't already, get into praying!

Verses 6-9

Jesus revealed the Father to his close disciples by everything he said and did. Their dim, black and white portable T.V. picture of God suddenly became glorious Technicolour, wide-screen, Nicam stereo, surround sound, etc etc! As they loved Jesus, they loved the Father too.

one another what I meant when I said, 'In a little while you will see me no more, and then after a little while you will see me'? ²⁰ I tell you the truth, you will weep and mourn while the world rejoices. You will grieve, but your grief will turn to joy. ²¹ A woman giving birth to a child has pain because her time has come; but when her baby is born she forgets the anguish because of her joy that a child is born into the world. ²² So with you: Now is your time of grief, but I will see you again and you will rejoice, and no-one will take away your joy. ²³ In that day you will no longer ask me anything. I tell you the truth, my Father will give you whatever you ask in my name. ²⁴ Until now you have not asked for anything in my name. Ask and you will receive, and your joy will be complete.

²⁵ "Though I have been speaking figuratively, a time is coming when I will no longer use this kind of language but will tell you plainly about my Father. ²⁶ In that day you will ask in my name. I am not saying that I will ask the Father on your behalf. ²⁷ No, the Father himself loves you because you have loved me and have believed that I came from God. ²⁸ I came from the Father and entered the world; now I am leaving the world and going back to the Father."

²⁹ Then Jesus' disciples said, "Now you are speaking clearly and without figures of speech. ³⁰ Now we can see that you know all things and that you do not even need to have anyone ask you questions. This makes us believe that you came from God."

³¹ "You believe at last!" Jesus answered. ³² "But a time is coming, and has come, when you will be scattered, each to his own home. You will leave me all alone. Yet I am not alone, for my Father is with me.

[33] "I have told you these things, so that in me you may have peace. In this world you will have trouble. But take heart! I have overcome the world."

Jesus sums up the chapter - "this world will give you grief, but I'm far greater than the world and you're on my team!!"

CHAPTER 17

Jesus prays for himself

After Jesus said this, he looked towards heaven and prayed:

"Father, the time has come. Glorify your Son, that your Son may glorify you. [2] For you granted him authority over all people that he might give eternal life to all those you have given him. [3] Now this is eternal life: that they may know you, the only true God, and Jesus Christ, whom you have sent. [4] I have brought you glory on earth by completing the work you gave me to do. [5] And now, Father, glorify me in your presence with the glory I had with you before the world began.

[6] "I have revealed you to those whom you gave me out of the world. They were yours; you gave them to me and they have obeyed your word. [7] Now they know that everything you have given me comes from you. [8] For I gave them the words you gave me and they accepted them. They knew with certainty that I came from you, and they believed that you sent me. [9] I pray for them. I am not praying for the world, but for

RE-CAP

Over the past three chapters Jesus has been talking with his disciples in private. Having said the last things he will say to them before his death, he lets them see him in action praying.

Unique moment

Remember, eternal life is more about the quality of life than the time span. Knowing God - having an intimate relationship with Jesus is the ultimate meaning to life.

Jesus brought God glory by revealing him so beautifully to the world. Jesus was now praying that God would restore to him the glory he had before he came to earth as a man. The Father, Son and Holy Spirit all work for each other's honour and glory.

This is especially true for Jesus, but also true for Christians. When I give my life to Jesus, I recognise that all I have belongs to him. Equally all that is his is mine - his love, joy, provision etc.

Jesus asks the Father to protect them - the name Jesus means "Saviour"

If the disciples were taken out of the world, how could they show people God's love? Jesus left us here to carry on his work, not to huddle up in a corner and wait for heaven!

those you have given me, for they are yours. ¹⁰ All I have is yours, and all you have is mine. And glory has come to me through them. ¹¹ I will remain in the world no longer, but they are still in the world, and I am coming to you. Holy Father, protect them by the power of your name—the name you gave me—so that they may be one as we are one. ¹² While I was with them, I protected them and kept them safe by that name you gave me. None has been lost except the one doomed to destruction so that Scripture would be fulfilled. — *Judas*

¹³ "I am coming to you now, but I say these things while I am still in the world, so that they may have the full measure of my joy within them. ¹⁴ I have given them your word and the world has hated them, for they are not of the world any more than I am of the world. ¹⁵ My prayer is not that you take them out of the world but that you protect them from the evil one. ¹⁶ They are not of the world, even as I am not of it. ¹⁷ Sanctify them by the truth; your word is truth. ¹⁸ As you sent me into the world, I have sent them into the world. ¹⁹ For them I sanctify myself, that they too may be truly sanctified.

²⁰ "My prayer is not for them alone. I pray also for those who will believe in me through their message, ²¹ that all of them may be one, Father, just as you are in me and I am in you. May they also be in us so that the world may believe that you have sent me. ²² I have given them the glory that

you gave me, that they may be one as we are one: [23] I in them and you in me. May they be brought to complete unity to let the world know that you sent me and have loved them even as you have loved me.

[24] "Father, I want those you have given me to be with me where I am, and to see my glory, the glory you have given me because you loved me before the creation of the world.

[25] "Righteous Father, though the world does not know you, I know you, and they know that you have sent me. [26] I have made you known to them, and will continue to make you known in order that the love you have for me may be in them and that I myself may be in them."

Jesus is committed to work with his church. His love will fill his people. The day will come when people will look at the church and say **"these guys remind me of Jesus!"** – he will be seen in us.

Quick definition:
"**Church**" those Jesus has called out from the world, ie Christians.

It has nothing to do with buildings!

High Fibre?

Jesus is praying for the future now - praying for us 90s disciples!

Jesus knew that all kinds of divisions would open up in his church as time went on. It's really sad to see how people who claim to love the same Jesus can treat each other so badly at times!

Throughout history the so-called church has been responsible for great self-abuse, even murder.

The wonderful thing is, that if Jesus prayed it it will surely happen.

Therefore we can be certain that one day there will be complete unity in God's church. Jesus prays for the unity which he has with the Father to be in the church - that's a bit of a way off at the moment!

The unity will not be some wishy - washy, splishy - sploshy man-made stuff with no guts, but it will be the vibrant, dynamic unity which the Holy Spirit is already starting to bring! Ministers (vicars, pastors etc.) from all ends of the rainbow are finding a weird desire to meet together and be friends, all of a sudden! **Could it be happening?**

Unity is not uniformity, where we all wear the same lovely dark suits or fluffy hats! *Our Dave says: "Look at creation - it's incredibly varied, multicolour, no two blades of grass are the same, but it all fits together in beautiful unity."* The same God who designed the cosmos will mastermind the unity in the church his people!

"Jesus has been arrested!"

Chapter 18

When he had finished praying, Jesus left with his disciples and crossed the Kidron Valley. On the other side there was an olive grove, and he and his disciples went into it.

² Now Judas, who betrayed him, knew the place, because Jesus had often met there with his disciples.

³ So Judas came to the grove, guiding a detachment of soldiers and some officials from the chief priests and Pharisees. They were carrying torches, lanterns and weapons.

⁴ Jesus, knowing all that was going to happen to him, went out and asked them, "Who is it you want?"

⁵ "Jesus of Nazareth," they replied.

"I am he," Jesus said. (And Judas the traitor was standing there with them.) ⁶ When Jesus said, "I am" he, they drew back and fell to the ground.

⁷ Again he asked them, "Who is it you want?"

And they said, "Jesus of Nazareth."

⁸ "I told you that I am he," Jesus answered. "If you are looking for me, then let these men go." ⁹ This happened so that the words he had spoken would be fulfilled: "I have not lost one of those you gave me."

¹⁰ Then Simon Peter, who had a sword, drew it and struck the high priest's servant, cutting off his

The soldiers (possibly hundreds) with some of the temple guard and the Jewish leaders came to arrest this "dangerous man" Jesus!

Jesus reveals himself as God by using the same word as God used to name himself to Moses in Exodus Ch 3 vv14,15.

Good old Peter, ready for a heroic last stand! He could understand a bloody show-down, but he could not cope with what Jesus had in mind.

right ear. (The servant's name was Malchus.)

¹¹ Jesus commanded Peter, "Put your sword away! Shall I not drink the cup the Father has given me?"

¹² Then the detachment of soldiers with its commander and the Jewish officials arrested Jesus. They bound him ¹³ and brought him first to Annas, who was the father-in-law of Caiaphas, the high priest that year. ¹⁴ Caiaphas was the one who had advised the Jews that it would be good if one man died for the people.

¹⁵ Simon Peter and another disciple were following Jesus. Because this disciple was known to the high priest, he went with Jesus into the high priest's courtyard, ¹⁶ but Peter had to wait outside at the door. The other disciple, who was known to the high priest, came back, spoke to the girl on duty there and brought Peter in.

¹⁷ "You are not one of his disciples, are you?" the girl at the door asked Peter.

He replied, "I am not."

¹⁸ It was cold, and the servants and officials stood round a fire they had made to keep warm. Peter also was standing with them, warming himself.

¹⁹ Meanwhile, the high priest questioned Jesus about his disciples and his teaching.

²⁰ "I have spoken openly to the world," Jesus replied. "I always taught in synagogues or at the temple, where all the Jews come together. I said nothing in secret. ²¹ Why question me? Ask those who heard me. Surely they know what I said."

²² When Jesus said this, one of the officials near by struck him in the face. "Is this the way you answer the high priest?" he demanded.

(Luke 22:51 tells how Jesus healed Malchus' ear! - He could still think of being kind to his enemies when he's about to be executed!)

"Don't you realise I'm going through with what my Father has asked me to do?"

They first took Jesus to be tried by the Jewish leaders.

v15 The other disciple was probably John.
He never mentions himself by name, but pops in and out of the story throughout the book.

Notice how John uses the names of people involved - it would have been easy for his original readers to check on the facts.

Probably the worst moment of Peter's whole life! - Jesus had known Peter better than Peter knew himself!

The Jews would become "unclean" by stepping into the Gentile house.

Remember reading Ch 1 v11 "He came to that which was his own, but his own did not receive him."

²³ "If I said something wrong," Jesus replied, "testify as to what is wrong. But if I spoke the truth, why did you strike me?" ²⁴ Then Annas sent him, still bound, to Caiaphas the high priest.

²⁵ As Simon Peter stood warming himself, he was asked, "You are not one of his disciples, are you?"

He denied it, saying, "I am not."

²⁶ One of the high priest's servants, a relative of the man whose ear Peter had cut off, challenged him, "Didn't I see you with him in the olive grove?" ²⁷ Again Peter denied it, and at that moment a cock began to crow.

²⁸ Then the Jews led Jesus from Caiaphas to the palace of the Roman governor. By now it was early morning, and to avoid ceremonial uncleanness the Jews did not enter the palace; they wanted to be able to eat the Passover. ²⁹ So Pilate came out to them and asked, "What charges are you bringing against this man?"

³⁰ "If he were not a criminal," they replied, "we would not have handed him over to you."

³¹ Pilate said, "Take him yourselves and judge him by your own law."

"But we have no right to execute anyone," the Jews objected. ³² This happened so that the words Jesus had spoken indicating the kind of death he was going to die would be fulfilled.

³³ Pilate then went back inside the palace, summoned Jesus and asked him, "Are you the king of the Jews?"

³⁴ "Is that your own idea," Jesus asked, "or did others talk to you about me?"

³⁵ "Am I a Jew?" Pilate replied. "It was your people and your chief priests who handed you over to me.

What is it you have done?"

³⁶ Jesus said, "My kingdom is not of this world. If it were, my servants would fight to prevent my arrest by the Jews. But now my kingdom is from another place."

³⁷"You are a king, then!" said Pilate.

Jesus answered, "You are right in saying I am a king. In fact, for this reason I was born, and for this I came into the world, to testify to the truth. Everyone on the side of truth listens to me."

³⁸ "What is truth?" Pilate asked. With this he went out again to the Jews and said, "I find no basis for a charge against him. ³⁹ But it is your custom for me to release to you one prisoner at the time of the Passover. Do you want me to release 'the king of the Jews'?"

⁴⁰ They shouted back, "No, not him! Give us Barabbas!" Now Barabbas had taken part in a rebellion.

Pilate had lost all grip of what the truth was.

Trying to please people can do this to you!

No Fibre?

Bad Friday. The Jews had only one thing in mind - to have Jesus killed. They had no basis for a criminal charge against him which would stand up in court, nor did they have the power to execute anyone. So they brought him to Pontius Pilate.

Pilate was the Roman governor of the area, the man with the real power **(but read Ch 19 v 11!)** He is shown to be an unwilling "accessory" to Jesus' crucifixion. Although he could find nothing wrong with Jesus, he went along with the whole charade to satisfy the Jewish hierarchy! **He had no fibre! A bit of a jelly-belly really!**

Jesus

SENTENCED

to death

Then Pilate took Jesus and had him flogged. [2] The soldiers twisted together a crown of thorns and put it on his head. They clothed him in a purple robe [3] and went up to him again and again, saying, "Hail, king of the Jews!" And they struck him in the face.

[4] Once more Pilate came out and said to the Jews, "Look, I am bringing him out to you to let you know that I find no basis for a charge against him." [5] When Jesus came out wearing the crown of thorns and the purple robe, Pilate said to them, "Here is the man!"

Jesus suffered extreme physical, emotional and mental abuse at the hands of the brutal soldiers. Yet as Isaiah prophesied all those years before:

Isaiah Ch 53 v7

" *He was oppressed and afflicted,*
yet he did not open his mouth;
he was led like a lamb to the
slaughter,
and as a sheep before her
shearers is silent,
so he did not open his mouth. "

Jesus made no attempt to escape or defend himself, yet he had all the power in the universe at his fingertips!

⁶ As soon as the chief priests and their officials saw him, they shouted, "Crucify! Crucify!"

But Pilate answered, "You take him and crucify him. As for me, I find no basis for a charge against him."

⁷ The Jews insisted, "We have a law, and according to that law he must die, because he claimed to be the Son of God."

⁸ When Pilate heard this, he was even more afraid, ⁹ and he went back inside the palace. "Where do you come from?" he asked Jesus, but Jesus gave him no answer. ¹⁰ "Do you refuse to speak to me?" Pilate said. "Don't you realise I have power either to free you or to crucify you?"

¹¹ Jesus answered, "You would have no power over me if it were not given to you from above. Therefore the one who handed me over to you is guilty of a greater sin."

¹² From then on, Pilate tried to set Jesus free, but the Jews kept shouting, "If you let this man go, you are no friend of Caesar. Anyone who claims to be a king opposes Caesar."

¹³ When Pilate heard this, he brought Jesus out and sat down on the judge's seat at a place known as the Stone Pavement (which in Aramaic is Gabbatha). ¹⁴ It was the day of Preparation of Passover Week, about the sixth hour. ● ● ● ●

"Here is your king," Pilate said to the Jews.

¹⁵ But they shouted, "Take him away! Take him away! Crucify him!"

"Shall I crucify your king?" Pilate asked.

"We have no king but Caesar," the chief priests answered.

¹⁶ Finally Pilate handed him over to them to be crucified.

Jesus sets the record straight: God had appointed Pilate for this awful day!

The Jewish leaders had Pilate over a barrel as he could not allow himself to be seen to be disloyal to Rome.

The sixth hour is about noon. Jesus must have been totally exhausted, as he had been questioned throughout the night, flogged and tormented all morning.

All without food or water.

Total hypocrisy! The Jews openly hated the Romans.

The cross Jesus carried was a heavy beam which was to be fixed horizontally to the upright post. It was what his hands were later nailed to. Jesus collapsed under the weight of it *(see Mark Ch 15 v21)*, and a man named Simon of Cyrene was press-ganged into carrying it.

So the soldiers took charge of Jesus. [17] Carrying his own cross, he went out to the place of the Skull (which in Aramaic is called Golgotha). [18] Here they crucified him, and with him two others—one on each side and Jesus in the middle.

[19] Pilate had a notice prepared and fastened to the cross. It read: JESUS OF NAZARETH, THE KING OF THE JEWS. [20] Many of the Jews read this sign, for the place where Jesus was crucified was near the city, and the sign was written in Aramaic, Latin and Greek. [21] The chief priests of the Jews protested to Pilate, "Do not write 'The King of the Jews', but that this man claimed to be king of the Jews."

[22] Pilate answered, "What I have written, I have written."

[23] When the soldiers crucified Jesus, they took his clothes, dividing them into four shares, one for each of them, with the undergarment remaining. This garment was seamless, woven in one piece from top to bottom.

[24] "Let's not tear it," they said to one another. "Let's decide by lot who will get it."

This happened that the scripture might be fulfilled which said,

"They divided my garments among them
and cast lots for my clothing."

So this is what the soldiers did.

One of those obscure little prophecies which most would have overlooked until it happened!

[25] Near the cross of Jesus stood his mother, his mother's sister, Mary the wife of Clopas, and Mary Magdalene. [26] When Jesus saw his mother there, and the disciple whom he loved standing near by, he said to his mother, "Dear woman,

here is your son," [27] and to the disciple, "Here is your mother." From that time on, this disciple took her into his home.

[28] Later, knowing that all was now completed, and so that the Scripture would be fulfilled, Jesus said, "I am thirsty." [29] A jar of wine vinegar was there, so they soaked a sponge in it, put the sponge on a stalk of the hyssop plant, and lifted it to Jesus' lips. [30] When he had received the drink, Jesus said, "It is finished." With that, he bowed his head and gave up his spirit.

[31] Now it was the day of Preparation, and the next day was to be a special Sabbath. Because the Jews did not want the bodies left on the crosses during the Sabbath, they asked Pilate to have the legs broken and the bodies taken down. [32] The soldiers therefore came and broke the legs of the first man who had been crucified with Jesus, and then those of the other. [33] But when they came to Jesus and found that he was already dead, they did not break his legs. [34] Instead, one of the soldiers pierced Jesus' side with a spear, bringing a sudden flow of blood and water. [35] The man who saw it has given testimony, and his testimony is true. He knows that he tells the truth, and he testifies so that you also may believe. [36] These things happened so that the scripture would be fulfilled: "Not one of his bones will be broken," [37] and, as another scripture says, "They will look on the one they have pierced."

[38] Later, Joseph of Arimathea asked Pilate for the body of Jesus. Now Joseph was a disciple of Jesus, but secretly because he feared the Jews.

With Pilate's permission, he came and took the body away. ³⁹ He was accompanied by Nicodemus, the man who earlier had visited Jesus at night. Nicodemus brought a mixture of myrrh and aloes, about seventy-five pounds. ⁴⁰ Taking Jesus' body, the two of them wrapped it, with the spices, in strips of linen. This was in accordance with Jewish burial customs. ⁴¹ At the place where Jesus was crucified, there was a garden, and in the garden a new tomb, in which no-one had ever been laid. ⁴² Because it was the Jewish day of Preparation and since the tomb was near by, they laid Jesus there.

Dear old Nicodemus.
Still skulking around in the twilight zone! He obviously loved Jesus but had found it difficult to go public until now.

the
chapter 20
empty tomb

Sunday morning

Matthew, Mark, Luke and John all have different details to bring out about that amazing morning. They complement each other to build up a full picture. John's account is particularly vivid, because he was there in person.

Early on the first day of the week, while it was still dark, Mary Magdalene went to the tomb and saw that the stone had been removed from the entrance. ² So she came running to Simon Peter and the other disciple, the one Jesus loved, and said, "They have taken the Lord out of the tomb, and we don't know where they have put him!"

³ So Peter and the other disciple started for the tomb. ⁴ Both were running, but the other disciple outran Peter and reached the tomb first. ⁵ He bent over and looked in at the strips of linen lying there but did not go in. ⁶ Then Simon Peter, who was behind him, arrived and went into the tomb. He saw

the strips of linen lying there, [7] as well as the burial cloth that had been around Jesus' head. The cloth was folded up by itself, separate from the linen. [8] Finally the other disciple, who had reached the tomb first, also went inside. He saw and believed. [9] (They still did not understand from Scripture that Jesus had to rise from the dead.)

[10] Then the disciples went back to their homes, [11] but Mary stood outside the tomb crying. As she wept, she bent over to look into the tomb [12] and saw two angels in white, seated where Jesus' body had been, one at the head and the other at the foot.

[13] They asked her, "Woman, why are you crying?"

"They have taken my Lord away," she said, "and I don't know where they have put him." [14] At this, she turned round and saw Jesus standing there, but she did not realise that it was Jesus.

[15] "Woman," he said, "why are you crying? Who is it you are looking for?"

Thinking he was the gardener, she said, "Sir, if you have carried him away, tell me where you have put him, and I will get him."

[16] Jesus said to her, "Mary."

She turned towards him and cried out in Aramaic, "Rabboni!" (which means Teacher).

[17] Jesus said, "Do not hold on to me, for I have not yet returned to the Father. Go instead to my brothers and tell them, 'I am returning to my Father and your Father, to my God and your God.' "

[18] Mary Magdalene went to the disciples with the news: "I have seen the Lord!" And she told them that he had said these things to her.

The stone was massive and would have taken several men to roll it back from the entrance.

They believed that Jesus had risen, but did not understand. It often happens that way round with God - we experience something and understand what it's all about later!

Brains muddled, they didn't think to tell poor old Mary!

Mary is in such grief that even when she sees Jesus himself, she doesn't recognise him! Then he says her name! The most important event in history and Jesus overlooks the Jewish "male thing" and reveals himself to a woman. Nice one!!

Jesus would have loved to have spent time reassuring Mary, but he still had places to go and people to see.

Sunday evening

Jesus' new body is not subject to the limitations of his first one - he can appear in a locked room without opening the door! Pretty amazing. But he can be touched and he has scars so he's clearly not a ghost or apparition!

Totally Fibrous?

Seeing is Believing "without Faith it is impossible to please God," (Hebrews Ch 11 v6.) God always gets excited about faith! (Read Hebrews Ch 11.) Why is that? Think about it - if you can **prove** I did something, you don't have to **trust** my word when I tell you. Real relationships are all based on trust.

It would be so easy for God to **prove** to the world beyond any doubt that he is for real. But then no "faith" would be needed. Like a parent God wants his children to snuggle up to him because they are loved, not because they are forced into it.

At this moment in time we cannot see Jesus therefore we must have faith if we are to follow him.

[19] On the evening of that first day of the week, when the disciples were together, with the doors locked for fear of the Jews, Jesus came and stood among them and said, "Peace be with you!" [20] After he said this, he showed them his hands and side. The disciples were overjoyed when they saw the Lord.

[21] Again Jesus said, "Peace be with you! As the Father has sent me, I am sending you." [22] And with that he breathed on them and said, "Receive the Holy Spirit. [23] If you forgive anyone his sins, they are forgiven; if you do not forgive them, they are not forgiven."

[24] Now Thomas (called Didymus), one of the Twelve, was not with the disciples when Jesus came. [25] So the other disciples told him, "We have seen the Lord!"

But he said to them, "Unless I see the nail marks in his hands and put my finger where the nails were, and put my hand into his side, I will not believe it."

[26] A week later his disciples were in the house again, and Thomas was with them. Though the doors were locked, Jesus came and stood among them and said, "Peace be with you!" [27] Then he said to Thomas, "Put your finger here; see my hands. Reach out your hand and put it into my side. Stop doubting and believe."

[28] Thomas said to him, "My Lord and my God!"

[29] Then Jesus told him, "Because you have seen me, you have believed; blessed are those who have not seen and yet have believed."

[30] Jesus did many other miraculous signs in the presence of his disciples, which are not recorded in this book. [31] (But these are written that you may believe that Jesus is the Christ, the Son of God, and that by believing you may have life in his name.)

John's reason for writing the book was not to catalogue Jesus' miracles, but to show that Jesus is the Son of God, because by believing in him we have eternal life!

chapter 21
Fishy happenings & New Beginnings!

Afterwards Jesus appeared again to his disciples, by the Sea of Tiberias. It happened this way: [2] Simon Peter, Thomas (called Didymus), Nathanael from Cana in Galilee, the sons of Zebedee, and two other disciples were together. [3] "I'm going out to fish," Simon Peter told them, and they said, "We'll go with you." So they went out and got into the boat, but that night they caught nothing.

[4] Early in the morning, Jesus stood on the shore, but the disciples did not realise that it was Jesus.

[5] He called out to them, ("Friends,) haven't you any fish?"

"No," they answered.

[6] He said, "Throw your net on the right side of the boat and you will find some." When they did, they were unable to haul the net in because of the large number of fish.

It seems that the disciples were either strapped for cash and had to sell some fish, or feeling a bit...

in-between-jobs at the the moment.

The word is literally "boys", or "lads".

By now Peter is desperate to touch base with Jesus, to say something about the other night when he let his dearest friend and Lord down so badly!

Each time Jesus appeared to his disciples after he was raised from the dead, it was to teach them a new lesson. This time he was showing them the way to work for him! The work we do every day, even the things we are good at, are only fruitful (see Ch 15) if we are working with Jesus.

Working all night without Jesus is a very fruitless exercise!

⁷ Then the disciple whom Jesus loved said to Peter, "It is the Lord!" As soon as Simon Peter heard him say, "It is the Lord," he wrapped his outer garment around him (for he had taken it off) and jumped into the water. ⁸ The other disciples followed in the boat, towing the net full of fish, for they were not far from shore, about a hundred yards. ⁹When they landed, they saw a fire of burning coals there with fish on it, and some bread.

¹⁰ Jesus said to them, "Bring some of the fish you have just caught."

¹¹ Simon Peter climbed aboard and dragged the net ashore. It was full of large fish, 153, but even with so many the net was not torn. ¹² Jesus said to them, "Come and have breakfast." None of the disciples dared ask him, "Who are you?" They knew it was the Lord. ¹³ Jesus came, took the bread and gave it to them, and did the same with the fish. ¹⁴ This was now the third time Jesus appeared to his disciples after he was raised from the dead.

¹⁵ When they had finished eating, Jesus said to Simon Peter, "Simon son of John, do you truly love me more than these?"

"Yes, Lord," he said, "you know that I love you."

Jesus said, "Feed my lambs."

¹⁶Again Jesus said, "Simon son of John, do you truly love me?"

He answered, "Yes, Lord, you know that I love you."

Jesus said, "Take care of my sheep."

¹⁷ The third time he said to him, "Simon son of John, do you love me?"

Peter was hurt because Jesus asked him the third time, "Do you love me?" He said, "Lord, you know all things; you know that I love you."

Jesus said, "Feed my sheep. [18] I tell you the truth, when you were younger you dressed yourself and went where you wanted; but when you are old you will stretch out your hands, and someone else will dress you and lead you where you do not want to go." [19] Jesus said this to indicate the kind of death by which Peter would glorify God. Then he said to him, "Follow me!"

[20] Peter turned and saw that the disciple whom Jesus loved was following them. (This was the one who had leaned back against Jesus at the supper and had said, "Lord, who is going to betray you?") [21] When Peter saw him, he asked, "Lord, what about him?"

[22] Jesus answered, "If I want him to remain alive until I return, what is that to you? You must follow me." [23] Because of this, the rumour spread among the brothers that this disciple would not die. But Jesus did not say that he would not die; he only said, "If I want him to remain alive until I return, what is that to you?"

[24] This is the disciple who testifies to these things and who wrote them down. We know that his testimony is true.

[25] Jesus did many other things as well. If every one of them were written down, I suppose that even the whole world would not have room for the books that would be written.

Just so Fibrous?

vv15-19 Peter had denied Jesus three times, now Jesus asks him three times if he loves him. Jesus uses the word **"agape"** which means **selfless love**, (JB) like the love which God has for us. Poor broken Peter answers with the word "phileo" which means **friendship or affection** - he knows he cannot claim anything great any more!

The third time, Jesus uses "phileo" almost questioning if Peter was still his friend, Peter was hurt. It is never easy facing up to our failures, yet when Jesus had forgiven Peter, he never mentioned it again.

After each question Jesus tells Peter to feed his sheep (his disciples, young and old). He was saying **"for each time you failed, I forgive you: carry on with the new job I am giving you"**. Jesus refers to Peter's offer to die for him **Ch 13 v37**. Peter was to be crucified for his faith some time later.

John puts an end to rumours of his possibly very, very long life!

We have just skimmed the surface of Jesus' life... but what a life!

fortified with iron & vitamins

ooops!!

Bo

God's rescue plan

Sin is missing the mark: by a million miles!

- Everyone is guilty - Romans Ch 3 v23
- Sin separates us from God
  - Isaiah Ch 59 v2
- Sin = death = separation from God for ever! Romans Ch 6 v23
- Sin actively controls our thoughts and actions before the new birth.
  Romans Ch 1 v18

The future is not looking very bright so far!

What is being "born again"?

● The entry point into God's kingdom and into God's family, Ch 3 v5, page 12. ● It is a spiritual birth, Ch 3 v6, page 12. ● It is becoming a child of God, Romans Ch 8 vv15,16. ● It is the start of a totally new life, and the end of slavery to sin. Ch 3 v16, page 15.

See Eternal Life on page 16

n again

How do I do it?

• **Jesus** came as the "Lamb of God", as a substitute to take the penalty for our sin. **Ch 1 v29 page 8.**

• **Jesus** didn't come to rub it in, but rub it out!, Bringing freedom from the death sentence! **Ch 3 vv16-18 page 15.**

• **Jesus** came to bring real life! **Ch 10 v10 page 42.**

• **Surrender to Jesus** - Believing in him will require making him your boss. **Romans Ch 10 v9**

• **Own up to your sin, stop making excuses!**

• **Ask God's forgiveness -** Be specific where you can. **1 John Ch 1 v9**

• **Ask Jesus to fill you** with the Holy Spirit. N.T. **Acts Ch 1 v8**

• **Go public -** tell someone… everyone! **Ch 4 vv39-42 page 19.**

"Oi mate…"

JARGONBUSTE

JARGONBUSTER

saw Jesus coming towards him and said, "Look, the Lamb of God, who takes away the sin of the world! [30] This is the one I meant when I said, `A man who comes after

This is a **Jargon** word, which on the surface looks pretty harmless, but may not make any sense to you at all until now.

For the scholars among you – we've given you the transliteration of the original Greek word. Showing off really!!)

The **Jargonbuster** is in alphabetical order, sometimes showing the Greek word as well.
The New Testament was first written in Greek; but knowing that won't win you any more Brownie points!!

SIN – GREEK: Hamartia

The word means literally "missing the mark". In the Bible it means all that falls short of God's perfect standard. It is an active force, opposed to God, controlling our thoughts and actions before we are "born-again". All humanity is guilty of sin.

• • • • • • • • • • • ⟶

BAPTISE – GREEK Baptizo

To dip or immerse. Baptism is the first major act of obedience to Jesus after we choose to follow him. It is an event which not only symbolises the burial of the old sinful life but also unites the believer with Jesus' resurrection. (See Romans Ch 6 vv3-4)

BELIEVE – GREEK Pisteuo.

Believing in the sense used by John is not just a "yeah, o.k. man, I believe ya" type of thing. It is a strong conviction inside given by the Holy Spirit. (See also Faith JB) **Faith is something you would stake your life on.**

BLESSING – GREEK Eulogia

Literally means to speak well of. God's acts of kindness to us are often called blessings. When he blesses us he makes our whole lives rich and fulfilled. Blessings may be spoken over people, asking God's favour upon their lives.

BRIDE / BRIDEGROOM

The Church is sometimes called the **"Bride of Christ".** **Jesus is the bridegroom.** (See Revelation Ch 19 vv6-9)

CEREMONIAL CLEANSING

The O.T. Law had a strict code of ritual cleanliness. If you became unclean; say by contact with a dead person, a certain procedure would have to be followed to become clean again. (See Leviticus Ch 10 v10, Ch 11 to 15)

CIRCUMCISION (see also page 32)

Cutting off a Jewish boy's foreskin on his eighth day was a sign that he belonged to God's chosen people.

CHRIST – GREEK Christos

Means anointed one. Priests, kings and prophets were anointed with oil in the Old Testament as a setting apart for their important work. Jesus was anointed with the Holy Spirit in a unique way for the work he came to do. (Read Luke Ch 4 vv17-21)

CONDEMNED
The sentence for sin has been passed - separation from God for ever. Just as in a court of law "the accused" becomes "the condemned", so because of our sin, we have the sentence of death hanging over us - until we turn to Jesus.

COUNSELLOR – GREEK Parakletos
Means someone beside you to help you. Jesus uses it as a name for the Holy Spirit. By using this word he sheds a bit more light on what the Holy Spirit does. The word speaks of someone close by who gives help, comfort and counsel from God.

DEMON possessed – GREEK Daimonizomai
Demons are spiritual beings who work for the Devil. They have a certain amount of power to mess up people's lives, their behaviour and health particularly. Jesus kicked them out of people when he encountered them. The word "possession" suggests they have total control of a person but more often they affect a certain area of the life. They can be a real issue, but soon shift when Jesus shows up!

FAITH - GREEK Pistis - same root as "believe"
Faith is believing what God has said and acting on it, when we have no physical evidence. Handing over your life to God whom you cannot see requires faith. God loves it! (See Hebrews Ch 11 v6 and "Totally Fibrous" page 78)

The FATHER
All human fathers are at best a pale reflection of God the Father. He is revealed by Jesus' life: "Anyone who has seen me has seen the Father." (Ch 14 v9 page 58) The Father, Son and Holy Spirit are together God. (See Holy Spirit JB.) While they are equal, Jesus honours the Father as the head.

GLORY – GREEK Doxa
Has a number of meanings in the Bible. We experience God's glory when his power or character are seen or felt

with our natural senses. The word often refers to a supernatural brightness or splendour; but can also be used in terms of worship, eg **"give Glory to God"** (Ch 9 v29 page 36) meaning praise God.

GRACE – ᏩᎡᎬᎬᏦ Charis.
Grace is at the very core of the whole Bible. It means God's amazing kindness to people who deserve nothing. It cannot be earned: it is endless and wonderful and free!

Holy Spirit; or The Spirit – ᏩᎡᎬᎬᏦ Pneuma.
Pneuma is also translated **"breath"** or **"wind"**. The Father, Son (Jesus) and Holy Spirit together are God. They are totally one in heart and mind, honouring each other in everything. (See One and Only JB)
The Holy Spirit is unseen and powerful. He fills the believer with God's love and power, changing him from inside out to be like Jesus. (See "High Fibre" page 13)

HOSANNA
It is a Hebrew word meaning "save we pray". It became a useful thing to yell at religious celebrations, expressing praise to God.

JESUS
Jesus is a common Jewish boy's name ("Joshua" in Hebrew). It means "Jehovah (God) is Saviour".

JUDGMENT
The final separation by God of those who have followed Jesus and those who have rejected him. (See "Last Day" JB)

LAST DAY
The last day spoken of in the Bible is the **"Day of Judgment"**. It is the end of time, when God finally gathers those who have followed Jesus to be with him for ever. Those who have rejected him will be banished from his presence for ever - hell. The earth will be wrapped up to make way for the new one which God will create. (Read Revelation Ch 21 vv1-5.)

LEVITE
A member of the Jewish tribe of Levi. This tribe was specially set apart to work in the temple. Priests were from this tribe. They were all financially supported by the rest of the community.

LIGHT
Jesus came as a light to show what had been hidden - the truth about God. Before Jesus came the world was in spiritual darkness - unable to see the truth. We remain in darkness until we accept Jesus.

LOVE – ϤRϾϾK Agape
The Greek word used for the kind of love God has for us is **"agape"**. It expresses a selfless love not fully understood before Jesus came. (Read Ch 15 v13 page 60.) It is the love with which the Holy Spirit fills our hearts (Romans Ch 5 v5). For a good definition of agape read 1 Corinthians Ch 13.

MESSIAH
See Christ JB - Messiah is the Hebrew equivalent.

PATRIARCHS
Literally, the fathers of the Jewish nation: Abraham, Isaac and Jacob. (See Genesis Ch 12 v49.)

PHARISEE See also "who's who in the Bible" page 26.
Member of a right-wing Jewish religious sect. They prided themselves on strict observance of the Law - both the Law of Moses (O.T.) and a whole pile of stuff added on by generations of Rabbis (teachers).

RESURRECTION – ϤRϾϾK Anastasis
Means **"raising up"** - from being dead! It is not resuscitation, or just giving back life, but a totally new kind of body. (Try reading 1 Corinthians Ch 15 vv35 - 56!)
Life after death is absolutely central to the N.T. Jesus' resurrection is as important as his death. *He is well alive!*

RIGHTEOUSNESS

Heavy duty jargon, borrowed by Bill and Ted - **"Totally righteous dudes!!"** God is the only one who is totally righteous. He is absolutely just and true, through and through. It is because he is righteous that the penalty for sin must be paid. It was his amazing love which made him pay the price himself!!

SABBATH

The seventh day of the week - our Saturday. The Ten Commandments (the backbone of the Jewish law) required this day to be a day of rest from normal work. God rested on the seventh day of creation. It is to be a special day for time spent with God - it stops us from becoming workaholics and makes us rely on God as provider.

SALVATION

To be saved from eternal isolation from God. To be rescued from the penalty of sin. Jesus' death on the cross made salvation possible.

SANCTIFY – GREEK Hagiazo

Another major jargon word! It means to be separated from the evil ways of the world, kept clean and pure, exclusively belonging to God. It is a choice on our part: "I want to belong totally to Jesus, and to stay away from sin". We can never achieve "sanctification" without the Holy Spirit changing us inside.

SANHEDRIN

The supreme Jewish court made up of learned religious figures and legal experts.

SAVIOUR

Jesus - the one who does the saving!

SCRIPTURE

At the time of Jesus, only the Old Testament had been written. Jesus, and later on his disciples, all taught and quoted from the Old Testament as the Word of God. He came to throw new light on the Old Testament - in the light of Jesus it all makes sense. The New Testament is the writing of Jesus' followers. For the Christian now, both the Old and the New Testaments are "the Scriptures".

SIN – GREEK Hamartia

The word means literally **"missing the mark"**. In the Bible it means all that falls short of God's perfect standard. It is an active force, opposed to God, controlling our thoughts and actions before we are "born-again". All humanity is guilty of sin. (Read *"born-again"* page 82-83)

SYNAGOGUE

A place where Jews would gather on the Sabbath to hear the Law read and taught.

TESTIMONY

As in a court of law someone who has witnessed an event accurately describes what they have seen or heard.

THE ONE AND ONLY – GREEK Monogenes

Speaks of Jesus' totally unique relationship with God the Father. He is the Son and always has been. The relationship between the Father and the Son is eternal, with no beginning or end. The concept of God as "Three in One" is called the "Trinity". It is that the one God exists in three persons who are equal yet distinct. A bit tricky to get your head round!! (See also Holy Spirit and Father JB)

The WORLD – GREEK Kosmos

John uses the word which speaks of the order and structure of the world, not just the physical planet. It refers to sinful society and its value systems; to that which is temporary in contrast to God's kingdom which is eternal.

WORSHIP

The main word used for worship of God is the Greek: proskuneo, literally **"draw near to kiss"**! Worship is our expression of love, devotion and awe to God.